BODY TALK

Real Girls Ask Real Questions About
Love, Life and Everything In Between

BODY TALK

Real Girls Ask Real Questions About Love, Life and Everything In Between

ANJALI WASON

HARPER

First published in India in 2010 by Harper
An imprint of HarperCollins *Publishers*
Building No 10, Tower A, 4th Floor, DLF Cyber, City Phase II,
Gurugram 122002
www.harpercollins.co.in

6 8 10 9 7

P-ISBN: 978-81-7223-962-6
E-ISBN: 978-93-5029-307-2

Typeset in Ehrhardt MT Std11/15
InoSoft Systems

Printed and bound at
Replika Press Pvt. Ltd.

HarperCollins *Publishers*, Macken House, 39/40 Mayor Street Upper, Dublin 1, D01
C9W8, Ireland

Contents

Dear Reader,

Body Talk is a comprehensive, honest book that aims to tell you the truth about sex and your body. A few years ago, I started interviewing young women from around the country on how they perceived sex, relationships and themselves. Over 400 women between the ages of 17 and 25 from across Delhi, Kolkata and Mumbai wanted to participate and talk about their hopes, dreams and anxieties. Together, they painted an enlightening picture of what it means to be a young middle-class woman in today's urban India – a world of gargantuan change.

Each girl I met was invited to ask an anonymous question about sex, love, life and everything in between. Four hundred questions later, this book – *Body Talk* – was born.

I received questions from young women wanting to know: *How do I tell my parents about my boyfriend? How do I use a condom? Can you get pregnant from oral sex? How do you have sex? How do I know if I'm gay? How can I build my self-esteem?* Within the pages of this book, you will come across these real questions asked by real girls, girls just like you – and *Body Talk* aims to answer all of these difficult questions.

While *Body Talk* is not confined to matters of sex and sexuality – we talk about family, friendship and acne among countless other things – sex is a very important aspect of the book. And I'm not just talking about the mechanics of reproduction and your period cycle, but that whole range of confusing personal and emotional issues that sex entails.

Sex is both dangerous and pleasurable, but because of the moral and medical issues associated with it, as well as its potentially life-changing implications, most books tend to focus only on its 'danger' aspect. They ignore the fact that women have desires and crave sexual pleasure and, as a result, don't dig deep enough to give you useful, real-world knowledge about sex.

Body Talk is about real life, a world in which everyone – and I mean *everyone* – has questions about love, life and sex. This book doesn't just give you the facts – this is not a biology textbook. It won't tell you what's right and wrong – it's not a book on morals. *Body Talk* is here to help you question, challenge, discover and explore the complexities of your body, your mind, your emotions and your relationships with other people.

You can use the book in any way you want – start from the beginning, turn to a random page, or search the index or table of contents for a topic that interests you. (But make sure you read Chapters 7 and 8 which discuss protection, STDs and all the stuff you need to know before you decide to have sex.) Check out the resources section for information on websites that can guide you through stressful times and the phone numbers you can call when you need a friendly ear.

The funda of this book is quite simple. Every society has its own ideas of what young women should and shouldn't do, or even can and cannot do. But increasingly, women are pushing sexual, emotional, physical and societal boundaries or doing away with them altogether. To remain happy and healthy, it is important to arm yourself with as much knowledge as possible. We all make mistakes along the way, but I hope this book helps you to feel less alone in the confusing wide world of life, love and sex.

And don't forget to check out our website: www.bodytalkindia.com, where you can contact us with your own questions, read what other people are saying, and find out more about your body and sex.

Anjali Wason

One

WHAT DO I LOOK LIKE?

Have you ever wished you had a smaller butt or skinnier arms? Or that your hair was long and straight? Ever worried that you were too large, too small, too tall, too skinny, overweight, not fair enough, too dark?

Unfortunately, none of us is a 100 per cent happy with the way we look. Ever wondered why you feel this way? Why can't we just look in the mirror and be happy with the person we see?

From an early age, we are taught that as women we need to look and act in a certain way. We should be fair, dainty, feminine homemakers, determined to please our men. But the only place where young women look uniformly slim-hipped, pert-breasted, clear-skinned, shiny-haired, long-legged and perfectly composed at all times is in the media – in films, magazines and on television.

One of the first things I learnt when I was writing this book was that no two women are the same. Each one of us has a different set of ideas, a different set of worries, a different set of circumstances. Just take a look at the women around you: some are tall, some short; some worry about money, some worry about grades; some have their whole future mapped out, some are more carefree; some have tons of freedom, some have none at all. Just as we are different on the outside, we are different on the inside too. We have thoughts that are unique to us which have nothing to do with what we look like on the outside.

This chapter looks at our bodies and the way we feel about them. We will learn how to ignore media images and pressure from the advertising industry. We will talk about breaking down the common stereotypes society has about women and learn to appreciate the beautiful and unique things about ourselves and about each other.

Self-Esteem

Self-esteem is the term we use to describe how we feel about ourselves. Having high self-esteem is when we like who we are and what we look like. We accept that there are good and bad things about our personality and appearance but we love every part of ourselves. Having low self-esteem is when we don't feel sure of ourselves. We tend to focus on our flaws and find it hard to accept compliments.

Low Self-Esteem

Think of a girl you know. Now imagine being really mean to her, laughing at her when she says the wrong thing, never forgiving her when she makes a mistake, telling her she looks horrible in red and getting angry when she does something embarrassing. A nasty way to treat someone, right? You're probably thinking, 'I would never treat someone like that!' Well, I've got news for you – this is how most of us with low self-esteem treat ourselves!

Causes of low self-esteem

Many of us experience low self-esteem at some point in our lives. There is no single thing that triggers low self-esteem – it's different for everybody, but these are a few common reasons that help explain why some of us have low self-esteem.

Comparison: Being compared to your siblings, cousins and friends can make you feel like you are not as good as they are.

Verbal Abuse: Constantly being told that you are fat, stupid or ugly is hard. If someone in your life repeatedly puts you down, it's hard not to start believing they are right after a while.

Being Let Down by the People You Trust: If someone whose opinion is really important to you, like your mother, father or best friend, suddenly says something negative about you, it can be heartbreaking and damage your self-esteem.

How Can We Build Self-Esteem?

'How do I build my confidence?' Sweetie

Having high self-esteem means you love yourself no matter what. You can still have a bad day that draws you to tears but you put things in perspective and realize it is just *one* day. Having high self-esteem is hard, and many women struggle with different insecurities their whole lives. Society has unwritten rules about how we should look or act in order to be considered cool or feminine, and this can put a lot of pressure on us without our realizing it. Many of us compare ourselves to our mothers or our friends and convince ourselves that we are not as good as they are or want us to be.

But there are some very tangible things you can do to boost your self-esteem and learn how to love yourself.

Cherish Yourself: Make a list of the things you love about yourself. Are you funny? Are you a good cook? Can you read fast? Do you have shiny hair? Are you considerate of people's feelings? Now look at what you wrote down. This is how beautiful a person you are. If you saw these traits in another person, you would think they were beautiful, right? So why not think of yourself as beautiful too? Make the list every day and add something new each time.

Be Positive: Look in the mirror every morning and say out loud, 'I am going to have a great day, I am a beautiful person inside and outside.' Positive reinforcement can work wonders. Or if it seems like you are having one of those days, you know, the ones where everything seems to be going wrong – you're late for class; you left your phone on the bus; you tore your kurti getting off the bus – try and take a deep breath and realize that this is just one bad day. Tomorrow is a new day and a chance for things to go right again.

Find Time for You: Make sure you have enough time to do the things you truly love. All the people and things in our life demand our time. Maybe your mother needs help in the kitchen every night or your homework takes up the whole evening. Or your friend needs you to go shopping with them. It's important to do these things too but you must also make time for yourself, to read a book, go shopping, dance, play badminton, swim – whatever it is you enjoy doing. Find at least an hour every day that's dedicated to you, and if that proves too difficult, start with fifteen minutes.

Exercise: Regular exercise can actually increase your positivity and make you feel great about yourself. Try and build some sort of exercise routine into your life. For example, instead of going to your usual bus stop, walk to the one that is a little further from your house or hostel and catch the bus from there. After lunch, take a walk with your girlfriends around campus or go to the local market. Join the local gym or take up swimming. Jog in your local park. Take an aerobics class. Regular exercise releases serotonin, which is the chemical in our brains that makes us happy. The more you exercise, the better you will feel about yourself.

Empowerment: Learning to say no is a very important part of building self-esteem. When someone asks you to do something you don't like or do not want to do, for instance, when a classmate asks to copy your homework or your brother wants to borrow money again, just say it – 'No.' Now ask yourself, how did that feel? Good, right? You are back in control of the situation and had the courage and power to say no.

Learn to Accept Compliments: If someone says, 'You're so good at maths,' reply with a simple thanks. And internalize the compliment – think about the compliment and let it be a part of you.

Don't Put Yourself Down: Don't say things like 'I have fat legs' or 'I wish I was better at maths'. You're just reinforcing the negativity to yourself. Besides, it makes other people think it's okay to put you down.

Talk to Someone: Expressing your feelings and thoughts to someone you trust can help you work through self-esteem issues. Start the conversation by telling your friend/sister/mum that lately, you have been feeling a little bad about yourself and that you would like to talk about it. You might find that you are not the only one. Most of us have moments in our lives when we feel down on ourselves and knowing you are not alone can help you through the hard times.

Body Hair

We have hair on almost every part of our bodies – on our arms, legs, stomach, chin, upper lip, back and pubic area. Some hair is finer and less noticeable, like the hair on your stomach or on your breasts and some thicker and more noticeable like the hair on your arms. Body hair is nothing to feel embarrassed about and you shouldn't feel like you have to get rid of it to look attractive. Men don't shave their faces every day so why should we?

Having said this, if any of your hair is making you feel uncomfortable or self-conscious, you can get rid of it easily through the following methods:

Threading (winding a thin thread around the hair root to pull it out): This is relatively painless, harmless and is available in any salon across the country. It's best for small areas, like your upper lip or eyebrows, because it takes a while to pull out each hair (so it's not recommended for removing the hair around your vulva). The hair doesn't grow back for approximately ten days.

Waxing (applying hot wax to the hair and then pulling it off in one swift motion): This is a safe method and perfect for large areas like the legs or arms. The hair will not grow back for about two weeks. But if you have sensitive skin, waxing can be quite painful and can even burst blood capillaries close to the skin's surface. This usually goes away after a while but can cause some redness for up to a week.

Shaving (using a razor to cut off the hair at the skin's surface): The great thing about shaving is that you can do it in the privacy of your own bathroom. The down side with razors is that they can be harsh on sensitive skin, plus the hair grows back quicker (in 2-3 days). Make sure you apply a shaving cream or hair conditioner on the skin before you shave and change your razor after using it a few times to be extra safe. Never share your razor with someone else –

you could be putting yourself at risk for HIV. Shaving is recommended for your underarms or legs. Do not shave the hair on your face. It will grow back thicker.

Depilatory creams (applying a cream to the skin): These creams are now readily available in the Indian market and are a convenient way to remove hair for about ten days. They are best for large surface areas like legs or arms and are completely painless. Make sure you read the instructions and use a clock to measure how long you should keep the cream on. Don't estimate – keeping the cream on for longer than recommended can harm your skin. Never use one of these creams on your face or around your vulva. They contain strong chemicals and the skin in these areas is extra sensitive.

Bleaching (using a chemical to lighten the colour of the hair): Bleaching is recommended for small areas where you don't have heavy hair growth, like your upper lip, for example. Bleaching is painless (though you might feel a slight tingling) and lasts up to a month for some people. If you are doing this at home, try not to get the bleach on your skin.

Skin Tone

'Why do boys always prefer to marry fair-complexioned girls?' Lalita

Unfortunately, there is a national obsession with skin tone. This can be traced to class, caste and social issues. In other words, the whiter your skin, the richer you are, the more social status you have. No one has to say this explicitly for us to believe it. It's in our minds, our media, our society. We are taught this from the day we are born.

Challenging the obsession with skin tone isn't easy. But it is necessary. Rising above superficial differences in skin tone will only reap positivity in your life. The next time someone drops a casual (or not so casual) remark about your skin tone or the next time you find yourself making a passing remark about someone's skin tone, stop yourself and try to see past the surface of the skin. Paying attention to skin tone is an archaic, outdated notion that doesn't, or shouldn't, belong in twenty-first century urban India.

Learn to love yourself from within. You are a beautiful person regardless of the colour of your skin. Besides, who cares what boys like? You don't need a boy to tell you whether you are fair, attractive, thin or smart. Love yourself for who you are and try not to care what other people think.

Nowadays, there are creams and skin products that claim to make your skin lighter but these 'solutions' contain high levels of chemicals, including bleach. We've all seen the misleading ads on TV and in magazines promising that the cream will make you fairer and therefore more attractive to the opposite sex. In fact, research has shown that prolonged use of these products can actually damage your skin and in some cases even make it darker, and we do not recommend you use them.

Acne

Big, small, one large one on your chin, some on your cheeks, maybe a glowing red one on your back... yep, that's right, I'm talking about pimples. Some of us get them when we have our period, some of us get them once a year, and some of us have them all the time. Whatever the reason and however big and frequent, pimples can make us feel miserable!

But no matter how terrible you feel about your pimple, never, ever pick at it. Even if it's itching or burning or throbbing. Fiddling with your spot could result in a lifelong scar. Having said that, I know some of us just can't resist the urge to pop the spot. If you're one of these people, and you just *have* to burst it, make sure you wash your hands thoroughly, take a bit of clean tissue and use this to squeeze the area directly around the spot. Use an ear bud dipped in aftershave to clean the area around the spot. This will help stop the bacteria from spreading to other parts of your face.

If you can resist the urge to pop your spot, then try one of these suggestions to reduce the redness and prevent the next one from coming up and ruining your week:

1. Mix some nutmeg powder with a few drops of milk and apply it to the pimple using cotton wool. This will help reduce the throbbing.
2. Apply some redness-reducing eye drops on the spot. These eye drops are designed to reduce redness in the eye and will have the same effect on your pimple.
3. Before and during your period, snack on some nuts or fruit. Papaya is especially good for the skin so overload on this fleshy fruit.

4. Make sure you get your daily dose of fruits and vegetables. You should be eating at least five portions of each every day. Junk food is okay – once in a while – but our nanis and mummies also know a little about nutrition so do listen to them!
5. Drink eight glasses of water a day. This will keep your skin hydrated and flush out any toxins.
6. Use a good daily face wash that contains salicylic acid, which is hard on acne. Wash your face gently only once a day and pat it dry with a towel afterwards.
7. Apply a light lotion specifically designed for sensitive skin.
8. Don't touch your face unnecessarily during the day. Your hands pick up a lot of dirt and bacteria during the day and you don't want to transfer this to your face.
9. Exercise regularly. Sweating opens up your glands, allowing the toxins to leave your skin. Plus exercise boosts your immune system, keeping you in tip-top shape.
10. Stress can make you break out in acne. Make sure you find some time to relax and do the things you enjoy.
11. Try and get 7-8 hours of sleep every night. This allows the body to regenerate and repair itself.

If your skin doesn't improve in a month or so, and you are still fed-up with your spots, make an appointment to see your doctor. She might be able to recommend something stronger.

Body Image

'I love my body and accept it as it is.' Pooja

Great news! Like Pooja, many of us are happy with who we are and love our body. But a lot of us worry about things like our weight, the hair on our stomachs, the size of our breasts. Almost all of us will find something negative to say about our body, focusing on the bad parts and ignoring the good parts. It's easy to look around at your skinnier friend, your fairer cousin, the blemish-free actress, the model with the perfect butt, and feel like *she* has *the* perfect body. Hey, we all do it – comparing and contrasting constantly – *I wish I had arms that didn't look like tree trunks; my butt sags way too much; if only my breasts were bigger…*

Chances are, though, that your friend, cousin, even the model and actress are unhappy with their bodies in some way and probably look at you wishing they had your flat stomach, your voluptuous hips, your gorgeous eyes. You wish you had what they have and they wish they had what you have. So, what does this tell us? 'You always want what you can't have' or 'Beauty is in the eye of the beholder'. Yeah, yeah, yeah, you've heard all this before. But these age-old sayings, no matter how many times you've heard them before, hold invaluable pearls of wisdom for those of us who worry about the way we look. What is the pearl of wisdom, you ask? Yep, you guessed it. There is no such thing as the perfect body!

Now, we know it's not easy battling a negative body image, or helping to maintain a positive one with all the confusing, there-is-such-a-thing-as-a-perfect-body messages out there.

So here's a quick list of things that might help contribute to a negative body image. It's virtually impossible to shield yourself from all the scenarios we have listed below, but understanding their potential impact on your body image is an important step to bidding goodbye to self-criticism and saying hello to loving yourself the way you are.

Friends Offering Advice

Sometimes our friends might offer advice like 'You should only wear black, it makes you look slimmer'. This sort of comment might sound harmless but it can actually be quite damaging. You end up feeling like you are fat and should only wear black. Or maybe your friends make fun of your dark skin and you laugh along even though it hurts your feelings – you don't want them to think you don't have a sense of humour. Unfortunately, your friends will keep teasing you about these things unless you tell them it's not okay.

Learning From Those We Love

If your mum, older sister, cousin or aunt is constantly worrying about her appearance, dieting, looking at herself in the mirror or criticizing herself, chances are you will learn that it's okay to do the same to yourself. Ask your mum, sister or aunt where they learnt to criticize themselves like that. Is it something they learnt from their elders? If so, it's important to see that there is a pattern here, and it's also important that you break this pattern. Suggest to your mum/sister/aunt that she and you should both make an effort to say something nice about yourselves when looking in the mirror. Support and help one another on days when you feel low and can't think of anything nice to say about yourself.

The Media

Traditionally, the Indian idea of beauty has always centred around the voluptuous, curvy woman but this is changing dramatically and nowadays the pressure to be poker thin with a flat stomach is pretty high. These days you just have to turn on your TV, open a magazine or visit your local cinema to see a gazillion images of skinny, doe-eyed actresses with flawless skin. Now let's give ourselves some credit – we don't rush out of the cinema or shut the magazine, convinced that we will start resembling these actresses if we starve ourselves, bleach our skin or straighten our hair. But what a lot of us do is look in the mirror and compare ourselves with the image of the actress. 'Hmm, my acne marks haven't cleared up, my hair is frizzy, my teeth aren't as white as hers, my hips are so much bigger… ARGHH!'

At times like these, it is important to remind yourself that the film-star or model only looks the way she does because she has spent two hours getting her makeup and hair done, and she has some seriously expensive clothes on (which would make anyone look good). The photographer or director has spent two hours trying to get five good pictures; the lights in the studio would make even a toad look beautiful; and all photographs and movies are touched up to get rid of spots, wrinkles, flab and dark circles. So, comparing yourself to someone in a magazine or a movie is futile.

The Dieting Industry

'I want to look good, thin and beautiful like Aishwarya Rai or Priyanka Chopra'. Pinky

The dieting industry is designed to make money! So, without a single thought for your well-being or happiness, the advertisers and marketers behind the dieting business will just try to sell you a product. They manipulate your low self-esteem and take advantage of your negative body image to make sure their product flies off the shelf!

It's easy to believe the pretty, skinny lady in a magazine or on TV when she swears that the product she's selling really is different and really does work! But, but, but, it's super important to resist the dieting industry's empty promises. Because they are just that – empty. Ever heard of the saying, 'If something is too good to be true, then it is'? The same applies here. There is no such thing as a quick fix to losing weight – no easy pill, no pink tonic, no book, no mantra that will magically make your weight issues disappear.

But there are long-term, effective approaches to losing weight. If you're determined to shed some pounds, choosing a regime that places emphasis on exercise and eating the right foods is a much healthier way to get into shape and tone your body. And once you have chosen a routine that works for you, stick to it. Research shows that yo-yo dieting – when you stop and start diets frequently – can lead to more weight gain and health problems later in life.

Eating Disorders

'Will I ever become slim and how can I look thin?' Nikky

Eating disorders are still relatively uncommon in India but studies show that this is about to change. Anyone who has an 'uncommon' relationship with food, in other words, they either fixate on food or think constantly about their body and dieting, is regarded as having an eating disorder.

Generally speaking, an eating disorder is a physical sign of someone's inner problems and worries. Controlling their food intake or trying to control their physical appearance through food may be an attempt to better control their lives. There is also a strong correlation between eating disorders and low self-esteem. As their preoccupation with food continues, men and women who suffer from eating disorders might feel marginalized or 'cut off' from society. They might feel guilty about not 'being normal' or 'good' or ashamed of their physical appearance, which in turn might lead them to starve themselves (anorexia); throw up after eating (bulimia); compulsively eat (compulsive overeating); or eat excessively large amounts of food in a short time (binge eating).

The research on eating disorders is constantly throwing up new theories, and the reasons one might suffer from an eating disorder are complex and difficult to understand. But it's safe to say that eating disorders are linked to the mind and should be treated holistically and sensitively. We have outlined the most common eating disorders, followed by a general set of questions to give you an idea about what to do if you think you or someone you love might be at risk of having an eating disorder.

Anorexia nervosa

The most common eating disorder is Anorexia nervosa, which is when someone starves themselves, skipping meals whenever they can. People who suffer from anorexia look in the mirror and see themselves as fat even if they are drastically underweight. They might be extremely scared to put on weight and will lie to you about what they are eating and when. People who are anorexic might over-exercise, in other words, they may develop an unhealthy, excessive relationship with exercising.

Bulimia nervosa

Those who suffer from bulimia usually eat large quantities of food irregularly. This is followed by major guilt pangs, during which one feels that they have to make themselves throw up or remove the food from the system by using laxatives or by over-exercising. Like those who have anorexia, people with bulimia see themselves as fat whenever they look in the mirror and can be very unforgiving about their physical appearance.

Binge eating disorder

People who suffer from binge eating disorder typically eat an unusually large amount of food in a short period of time, usually to distract themselves from unhappy or negative thoughts. Unlike those with bulimia, binge eaters do not remove the food from their system and might gain weight rapidly. This weight gain in turn feeds their feelings of insecurity and inadequacy and leads them to further binge eat.

How do you know if you or a friend is suffering from an eating disorder?

If you answer yes to one or more of these questions, you could be suffering from an eating disorder.

1. Do you find yourself thinking about food all the time?
2. Do you feel guilty when you eat?
3. Do you see only fat when you look in the mirror?
4. Do you often skip meals?
5. Do you vomit after meals?
6. Do you exercise excessively?
7. Do you lie to yourself or to someone else about what you eat?
8. Do you think all your problems would disappear if only you were thin?

Getting help for an eating disorder

Talk to someone you trust, maybe your family doctor, your mother, a teacher or a friend. Admitting that you might be suffering from an eating disorder is an important and essential step to getting better, and it will help you cope with your worries and anxieties. Anorexia, bulimia and binge eating are all treatable disorders and with the right support and expertise, can be treated successfully. See the resources chapter at the end of this book for more information.

Gender

What is Gender?

We all know that boys and girls have different bodies – men don't give birth, women have periods. These are our biological differences. Gender is the word used to define the social and psychological differences between boys and girls, men and women.

Gender is something that is usually thrust upon us. Mainstream society makes generalizations about how men and women should act simply because of what they have between their legs. In other words, according to typical gender stereotypes, just because a boy has a penis, he should be 'masculine' – play cricket, never cry, only wear shorts and trousers. And because a girl has breasts and a vagina, she should be 'feminine' – be able to cook, be sweet, and want to have children. We use words like 'feminine' or 'masculine' to describe someone and make presumptions about them and the way they either fit into these categories or don't.

You aren't born with the idea that there is a 'masculine' or 'feminine' way to be. These are ideas that society thrusts onto you as you grow up. From the kind of clothes you wear to what toys you play with, to what kind of animals you like, you are squeezed into one of the two categories. We've all been there. Feeling like we should dress a certain way to assert our femininity, or being told repeatedly that we should act more like a girl – in other words, be dainty, quiet, cute and sweet. Boys also fall victim to these suffocating stereotypes. They're supposed to play sports, be masculine, brave, ambitious and loud.

If you're reading this and thinking – 'But I like to play cricket as well as cook, so what does that make me?' – then you are like most of us out there who feel constrained by the idea of gender. Gender implies that there are only two ways of existing in the world – as a girl or as a boy. The truth, however, is that most of us feel like we are somewhere in between. So you might like to cook but also enjoy a game of cricket. You may want to have children but also start your own business some day.

There are a set of unwritten messages that tell us how men and women should act. These expectations sometimes come from our families, our communities and often from within ourselves. These are our gender roles. Maybe your teachers pay more attention to the boys in your maths class than to the girls? Or your mum expects you to clear the table after dinner while your brother plays on the computer? From birth, these limitations on how we should be and act penetrate every part of our lives. But as we mature into adults, it is important to question these roles – and to realize that it is possible to exist outside these pigeonholes.

Think about Sunita Williams, the young astronaut who went into outer space as part of a NASA mission in 2007. Some people tell us that girls aren't supposed to be good at maths or science, right? Or brave and strong? Just one look at this pioneer proves them wrong. We don't have to fit into the accepted roles that society pushes on us – like being a teacher, a nurse, a mother or a wife. There are hundreds of examples around us to prove that women are more than capable of doing anything that men can do (and often even more). Countless women who have led successful lives come to mind, like Sonia Gandhi, Hillary Clinton, Benazir Bhutto, Nandita Das and Jhumpa Lahiri among numerous others.

Gender Strikes

Challenging gender roles in your family, school, community or culture takes a lot of effort and time. But the freedom to explore the world and get to know yourself without the constraints of gender seems worth fighting for. And there are a couple of things *you* can do to defy gender roles:

- Next time you find yourself making a presumption about someone based on the way they look, stop yourself. For example, many colleges have something called the 'sports crowd'. These girls tend to be good at sports, may have short hair and often 'dress like boys'. They are treated with indifference or disdain by some of the other groups in college. 'I know they're all lesbians,' said one Delhi University student. But just because you are into sports, cut your hair short or prefer to wear shorts, it doesn't mean you are a lesbian (and even if you are, that's okay too). Stereotypes and generalizations can be harmful and hurtful and only serve to make people feel isolated.
- Instead, try and think about why you feel this way. Is it society that makes you think this way? Or do you really believe that only boys should have short hair? Try to step out of this mindset and do something completely contrary

to what you might normally do. Befriend one of the girls from the 'sports crowd'. Join the sports team yourself.

- The world isn't going to change overnight. And neither are you. But every time you feel suffocated by gender roles, or find yourself making presumptions about someone based on their gender, or overhear someone saying something like 'I have never seen her wear a dress, she is such a tomboy!' *stop*, *think* and *challenge* yourself.

Transcending Gender

Gender, like sex, implies that the world is split into two types of people – men and women. But this is a restrictive lens through which to view the world. In fact, the world's population is made up of millions of people who do not identify with either sex or either gender. Here are examples of two communities who do not conform to either male or female genders:

Transgender: Someone who is anatomically (or biologically) of a certain sex (i.e. man or woman) but identifies better with the opposite gender is often referred to as transgender. Members of the transgender community can be straight, gay or bisexual. They simply choose to live their life by identifying with the gender they feel more comfortable with, rather than the gender that's associated with their biological sex.

Transsexual: Someone who has undergone surgery to change their anatomy to resemble the gender they identify with is called transsexual. In India, there are an estimated 200,000 male to female hijras, or transsexuals, who are men who have undergone surgery to become women.

What Do I Do if I Feel this Way?

There is no doubt that there are hefty social taboos around alternative gender communities. Like anything that strays from the norm, transsexual and transgender people are often treated with fear and disdain by mainstream society. Jokes are made, hurtful comments hurled and even violent acts committed against transsexual and transgender communities all the time.

Unfortunately, this might make it hard for someone who relates to or identifies with these communities, to come forward. You might be worried about how your family will react, how society will treat you. Fortunately, there are a lot of resources within the country, mainly in the big cities, that can help. Check out the resources chapter at the end of this book for a list of organizations that offer support, help and advice.

TWO

GETTING TO KNOW YOUR BODY BETTER

In this chapter and in this book, we want to get to the nitty gritty of what our body is made up of without worrying about auntyjis and the moral brigade. It's perfectly natural to be curious about your genitals, breasts or any other part of your body. In the next few pages, you will see that lots of girls have questions about their bodies, like – *My boobs are uneven, what should I do? Are orgasms normal? I have had my period for a month continuously… is something wrong?* The answers to these questions aim to shed some light on things you might have been wondering about, like – *What exactly happens when you get your period? What is the difference between the vagina and the vulva? What is the vaginal opening? When do your breasts stop growing?*

How does a girl masturbate? How does a boy masturbate?

Yes, we also talk about masturbation and orgasms and wet dreams – and you will learn that it is natural and common to want to touch yourself sexually, to have desires and to feel turned on.

Understanding your body, taking the time to explore it and marvel in it, is a priceless part of being a woman. So take your time, find your way through these pages, and by the end, you might discover a thing or two about yourself.

Your Breasts

'My boobs are not fully developed – what can I do?' Hemani

Developing more slowly than your friends is tough. But it's important to remember that we all come in different shapes and sizes and develop at different rates. While some women stop developing at 14, some do so at 18 and some at 21. Besides, even if you do find that you have small breasts, try and remember that the size of your breasts doesn't determine how interesting life is going to be.

Too small

'Many guys have told me I have small boobs. I feel so embarrassed about them.' Shazia

I know it's tough to shrug off someone's hurtful comments but these guys are just trying to push your buttons. The size of your breast is determined by how much fat tissue there is behind the breast. So, if you are a small girl, chances are that your boobs will be in proportion to your body size. Learn to love what you have and enjoy yourself no matter what size your breasts are.

Too big

'Are bigger boobs sexier than smaller ones? What do guys like the most?' Priya

All boobs are sexy! Some people find small breasts sexy, some find large nipples on small boobs sexy, some find large breasts and small nipples sexy. Boobs are boobs and the truth is that men and women find all breast sizes sexy. Not to mention, some people are more interested in your personality and what you have to say than in the size and appearance of your breasts. Most importantly, love yourself for who you are and what you have.

Uneven breasts

'I don't like my breasts coz I feel they are unequal.' Swati

It's very common to have one breast slightly bigger than the other. This is normally because they grow at different rates during puberty. Most breasts usually even out in a few years but if they don't, fret not. Remember that the unevenness is probably noticeable only to you.

How to Measure Your Bra Size

What do I need?

Just a tape measure – use the inches side.

What do I do?

Wrap the tape measure around your body, just underneath your breasts. Make sure your arms are down and that the measuring tape is quite tight. What does it say on the tape measure in inches? Round this number to the nearest **even** number. For example, if you measure 32.6 inches, then round off to 32 inches. If you measure 31 inches, then round off to 32 inches, etc. This is called your band size.

Now you need to measure your cup size. Run the tape measure loosely around where your breasts are the fullest, in other words, make sure the tape measure covers your nipples. What does it say on the tape measure? Round this number to the nearest whole number.

Now subtract your first measurement from the second one to get your cup size. For example, let's say your first measurement under your breasts was 34 inches and your bust size measurement was 36 inches. Your cup size will be 36 inches minus 34 inches. Once you have this number, use the chart below to get an indication of your cup size. (This method may be less accurate for larger breasts.)

1 inch or less = AA cup

1 inch = A cup

2 inches = B cup

3 inches = C cup

4 inches = D cup

5 inches = DD cup

6 inches = E cup

7 inches = F cup

8 inches = FF cup

9 inches = G cup

How do I know if I have the right size on?

Are you able to run your fingers around the inside of the bottom of the bra? If not, your bra is too small for you. Do the straps leave marks on your skin when you take off your bra? If so, your bra is too small for you. Go up a bra size but down a cup size. For example, if you are wearing a 34 C and find it's too tight, change to a 36 B.

What kind of bra should I buy?

There are all sorts of bras out there – sports bras, padded bras, demi-cup bras, full-cup bras and underwire bras are the most common but there are countless variations. Try out a few to see what feels most comfortable. You might also find that different bras work for different outfits/activities. To get you started, here is a quick rundown of some common types of bras:

- Padded bras add cushion and can make your breasts appear bigger than they are.
- Demi-cups will cover your nipple area but leave the top, fleshy part of your breast exposed.
- A full cup covers your entire breast.
- Sports bras are usually made of breathable, stretchy fabric and offer good support for your breasts while you exercise.
- Underwire bras have a thin wire that offers a comfortable 'shelf' for your breasts. Some women swear by these bras, believing that the underwire offers a lift to their breasts but others find them uncomfortable.

Things to remember before you buy a bra

- When trying on a bra, loosen the straps – does the bra still support your breasts? This is a good sign.
- If your breasts are slightly uneven, get a bra that fits the bigger breast.
- Remember that bra sizes change over the years. Your breasts become fuller or smaller depending on your weight and before and after your period.
- Different brands have different measurements. So, if you find a bra that is comfortable, buy a couple.
- Don't buy the wrong size just because it's on sale.

Your Bits and Bobs

Many of us worry whether everything is okay down there – *Should my vagina look like that? Smell like that?* But every vagina looks, smells and acts uniquely. Just like no two penises act, hang or look the same. Everyone is built differently.

Here is a quick run down of a woman's and man's reproductive bits and bobs so that you are one step closer to understanding the human body.

Women

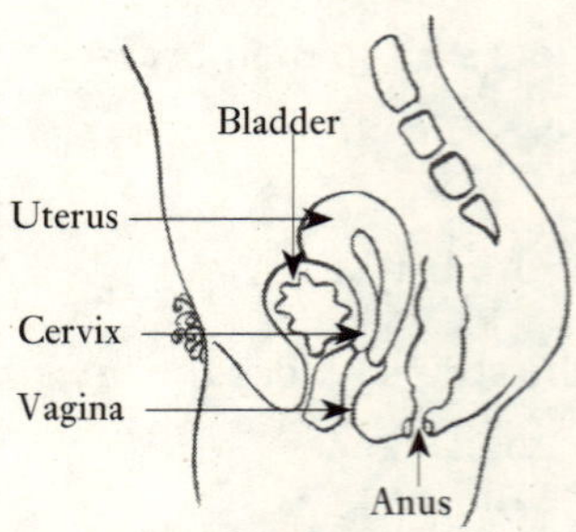

FEMALE GENITALS

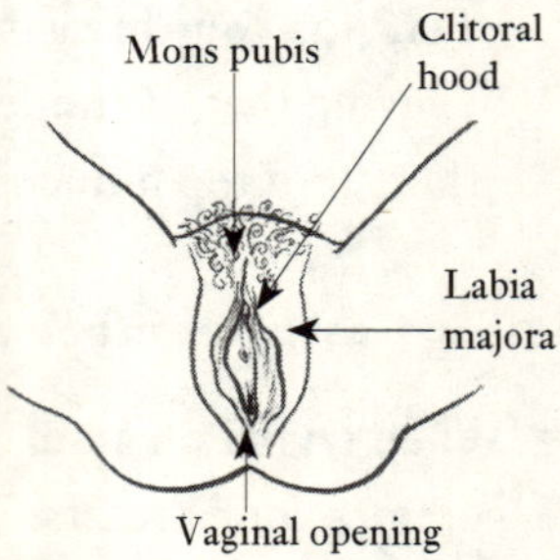

VULVA

Vulva: This is the part of the vagina you can see and includes the labia minora and labia majora.

Urethral opening: This is the hole through which urine comes out. It is connected to the bladder by a small tube.

Vaginal opening: The vaginal opening is an elastic passage that stretches and contracts according to its role. One of the functions of the vaginal opening is during childbirth. Through this channel, the baby is squeezed from the womb into the world. During penetrative sex, the vaginal cavity stretches to fit a penis. The vaginal opening doesn't lose its elasticity during sex and will return to its normal size after intercourse.

Labia majora: These are the thickish, dark-coloured lips that run along the outside of your vagina. The labia majora shield your inner genitals and keep moisture locked in the vagina. They have lots of nerve endings that help you get aroused during sexual activity.

Labia minora: Like the labia majora, the labia minora act as a barrier to the urethral and vaginal openings. They have more nerve endings and blood vessels than the labia majora, are over-sensitive and even a little stroking of the labia minora can make you feel super turned on. It's perfectly normal for your labia minora to hang out of your labia majora and be visible.

Clitoris: The only known function of the clitoris is sexual pleasure. It is very sensitive to touch and when stimulated in the right way, can make you feel amazing. When you are aroused, the clitoris becomes erect, although it's not visible outside the body.

Clitoral hood: The clitoral hood protects the clitoris glans, a pea-sized part of the clitoris that's very sensitive to touch. To achieve sexual pleasure, many women like to be rubbed gently on the clitoral hood and this, in turn, stimulates the clitoris.

Mons pubis: This is the mound (or bump) directly above your vulva and is usually covered in pubic hair. Your mons pubis can also be sensitive to touch and, if rubbed gently, can stimulate the clitoris below it.

Men

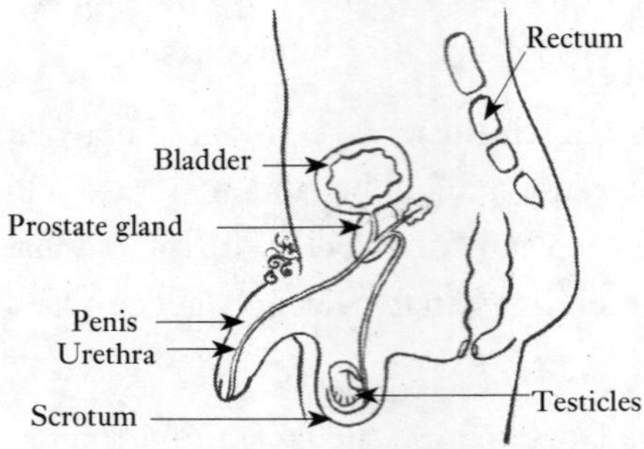

MALE GENITALS

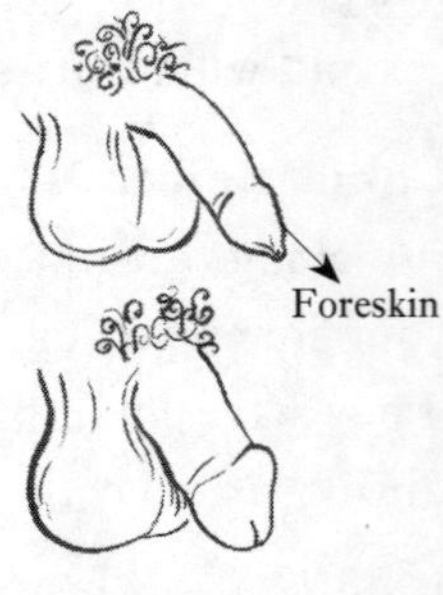

PENIS

Scrotum: The scrotum is a loose sac of skin that holds the testicles. It is made of the same tissue as the labia majora on a woman and can be very sensitive.

Testicles: The testicles are responsible for making testosterone, the main male sex hormone, and for producing sperm. These oval organs manufacture billions of sperm in one lifetime or about 1,000 sperm per second. A man's testicles are very sensitive and delicate. When a man gets kicked in the balls or something hard strikes his genital area, as you may have seen in movies, he may double over in pain. This is because the testicles are very fragile and can really hurt a man if handled roughly.

Sperm: Individual sperm is so small it can't be seen by the naked eye and yet it is the key ingredient in getting a woman pregnant. Sperm is produced in the testicles and transported to the urethra through a complex collection of tubes behind the testicles in preparation for ejaculation. When a man ejaculates, he emits a white, thickish liquid called semen, which contains hundreds of thousands of sperm.

Urethral opening: Men pee and ejaculate from the urethral opening.

Penis: This is the main male sex organ and lies limp unless sexually stimulated. If a man is sexually stimulated, blood rushes into internal compartments in the penis and makes it swollen, erect or 'hard'. It is possible to have sex even if a man's penis is not completely hard or erect, although this might make penetration a little more difficult.

Foreskin: The foreskin is the layer of skin covering the penis. Some men have their foreskins removed when they are babies. This is called circumcision.

Periods

When Does Your Period Start?

Many of us started our periods when we were about 13 or 14 years old. However, it really depends from person to person. Some girls start as early as 9 or 10 and some as late as 17 or even 18. But if you have not started your period by the time you are 16 or 17, it's best to get it checked by a doctor. Sometimes stress or an unhealthy diet can delay the onset of your period. Although this is no big deal, it's best to get it checked.

What Is a Period?

Every month, during a process called ovulation, an egg (ovum) matures and travels out of one of your two ovaries. Your ovaries are located in your lower abdomen and hold all the eggs (ova) you will ever have in your lifetime.

Once the egg leaves one of your ovaries, it moves through your Fallopian tubes towards your uterus. Your body receives a signal that it's time to start building a thick lining made up of blood and tissue inside your uterus. If your egg is fertilized by sperm, the lining will act like a protective bed for the egg as it matures into a foetus.

If there is no fertilization, your body has no need for this thick lining. So it expels the blood and tissue it gathered in the uterus through your vagina over 3–7 days, and this is called your period.

Your Period Cycle

Every month, approximately 14 days after the first day of your last period, during a process called ovulation, an egg is released from one of your ovaries.

This itsy-bitsy egg (about the size of a pinhead) travels to the Fallopian tube and your body starts to build a thick lining of blood and tissue in your uterus, preparing for the egg.

You are now at your most fertile. You might find a slippery, stretchy, clear or slightly yellow mucus in your panties. This is called 'fertile' mucus and is used by the body to carry sperm.

Your body creates small waves, like tiny vibrations, that push the egg towards the uterus.

If your egg meets a sperm while moving down the Fallopian tube, the sperm will push its way into the egg. This is called fertilization.

The fertilized egg is pushed into the womb, where it nestles in the thick lining. You are now pregnant. This egg will grow into a baby in nine months.

If the egg isn't fertilized, about nine days after ovulation, the thick lining of blood and tissue is expelled from the vagina over several days. This is called a period.

Period Pains

About 90 per cent of women experience discomfort or become irritable just before and during their period. This is brought about by hormones that fluctuate sharply around your period. Most of us experience some pain on and off about a year after our first period and this can last for a few years. But for some of us, period pains can appear years after our first period and continue throughout our lives.

My Period's Coming

Your body gives you various signs that tell you your period is due. Here are some of the symptoms along with some simple ways to help you deal with them.

SYMPTOMS	CURE
Pimples/Acne	Take some vitamins, especially Vitamins E and B.
Irritability/ Moodiness	Accept that it's okay to be a little moody sometimes. Spend a little more time with yourself so that you don't have to worry about upsetting anyone.
Increased sensitivity	It's okay to cry sometimes. Keep a journal of things that hurt you during this period and read it in a few days. Do you still feel the same way about the things you wrote down? Chances are, you don't.
Bloated stomach	Put a hot water-bottle on your lower stomach or lie on your back and hug your knees for ten minutes.
Cramps	Take a painkiller – something like an aspirin is okay once in a while. But be careful and only take it if you are in a lot of pain. Masturbation leading to orgasm also helps relieve tension and can reduce cramps.
Depression/Lack of energy	Take a long, warm bath or shower and listen to your favourite song. Make sure you are good to yourself and do something you enjoy, like watch a movie or go shopping.

A sudden sweet tooth	Don't give into this. The craving will only last a few minutes and in the long run, the sweets will only make you feel worse. Instead, have some fruit or some dates.
Sore breasts	Put on a bra first thing in the morning which will stop your breasts from jiggling up and down when you walk, causing pain.
Clumsiness	Get some exercise. Go for a short jog or play some badminton. Something light and fun that will get your mind off your discomfort.

Problem Periods

Sometimes high levels of stress, like a death in the family or exam stress can change the flow of your period. At other times, simple things like an increased temperature in the air can delay your period. For example, when the summer first hits, the sudden heat can affect your cycle and make your periods heavier and longer. Having said that, if you find there is a significant change in your cycle, for example, if your periods are much heavier or lighter than usual, you should see your doctor straightaway.

Heavy periods

If you've noticed that your period has gotten heavier in the last few months, go and see a doctor as soon as possible. Heavy periods mean you are losing a lot more blood than you used to. Before your body adjusts to this, you may experience problems like low energy or dizziness.

Light periods

If you have noticed that your periods have become lighter than usual over a few months, go and see a doctor. You might not be eating enough, or something stressful in your life might be stopping you from having a regular period.

Missed periods

The first question to ask yourself is – have you been sexually active in the last few weeks? If so, you could be pregnant. Did you use protection? If not, you could be pregnant. You will always be at risk for pregnancy if you have engaged in any sexual activity and, unfortunately, not all protection is foolproof, even if you used it correctly.

If you answered yes to having sexual contact with someone in the last few weeks: Go to your doctor as soon as possible. Don't be worried – all doctors have to keep everything you tell them confidential. But if you don't feel comfortable going to your usual doctor, see if you can find a new one or ask one of your friends to recommend a doctor. See Chapter 8 for more information on how to talk to your doctor.

Or you could buy a pregnancy test from a chemist. Pregnancy tests are very easy to take (you usually just have to pee on them) and cost about Rs 48 for two. They are readily available and will tell you within two minutes whether you are pregnant or not. It's best to take the test approximately 5-6 days after your missed period. Ask a friend to stay with you for some support while you take the test. If you find the test comes out positive, turn to Chapter 6 for advice on what you can do. Remember, pregnancy tests are not always accurate so take another one in a few days just to be sure.

If you answered no to having sexual contact with someone in the last few weeks: Are you eating properly? Are you dieting excessively? Or training for something like a marathon? Have you recently changed schools? Or moved to a new city? Did someone close to you pass away? Are you under a lot of pressure at school? Is someone touching you in a place you don't want to be touched?

These are just some of the reasons why we might miss a period altogether. Your body is just responding to the tension in your mind. Try speaking to someone about what's going on and see your doctor about getting some medicinal help.

Pads or Tampons?

Pads

Pads, or sanitary towels, are long, cushioned layers of cotton-wool padding which we can put in our panties to catch the blood from our period. You can choose from light, medium and heavy pads, depending on the type of flow you get. Make sure you change your pads regularly to prevent any odour and discomfort.

Panty liners

Panty liners are basically thin pads. They are usually used at the end of a period to catch the lighter flow. They help you keep fresh as you can change them as often as you like.

Advantages of wearing a pad

- They are hassle-free
- They are available everywhere
- There are many different kinds to choose from
- They are cheap

Disadvantages of wearing a pad

- They can feel uncomfortable, especially when it is hot
- You cannot swim with a pad on
- You can't wear super-tight clothing

Tampons

Tampons are tightly-packed three inch tubes of cotton. When inserted into your vagina, they absorb the blood flow from your period. They are available in heavy, medium or light, depending on your flow. You should change your tampon every 4–5 hours, regardless of whether you think it is filled or not.

How to insert a tampon

Most tampons come with an applicator, which is a plastic tube around the tampon that helps you insert it into your vagina.

1. Make sure your hands are clean.
2. Put one of your legs up on the toilet seat or on the edge of the bathtub so that your vagina opens up a little.
3. Take a deep breath to relax yourself. Tension will cause your muscles to tighten, making the process a lot harder.
4. Slide the tampon (with the plastic applicator still attached – do not try to separate the two) into your vaginal opening at a slight upward angle. Once the tip is inside, push upward and backward, towards your bum.
5. Push gently until you feel it stop by itself. Do not push any more. If you buy a tampon without an applicator, then you should use your fingers to push the tampon into your vagina. A tampon can never be lost inside of you so don't be worried about how far you're pushing it.
6. The applicator, which is the plastic bit you have been holding onto, should slide out easily. Throw it in the bin.
7. The string should hang down between the vaginal lips.
8. Put your leg down and walk around a little. How does it feel? If it's inserted correctly, you should not be able to feel the tampon inside you. If you can feel it, take it out and try again with a fresh tampon.

9. Don't experiment with a tampon when you do not have your period. Your vagina is not lubricated enough, and it will be hard to tell whether it feels comfortable or not.
10. To remove the tampon, pull lightly on the string hanging down.

How do you throw away a tampon?

Never flush a tampon down the toilet. Like a pad, wrap it in some tissue or newspaper and throw it in the bin.

Advantages of wearing a tampon

- You can swim or participate in any sport you want even when you have your period
- You can wear tight clothing
- Tampons, if inserted correctly, are very comfortable and easy to use

Disadvantages of wearing a tampon

- They are not so easily available across India
- They are slightly more expensive than pads
- The risk of TSS (Toxic Shock Syndrome)
- Remembering to change it every four hours, whether it is full or not
- You can't sleep with a tampon inside you

TSS (Toxic Shock Syndrome)

TSS is a rare condition that can be caused by keeping your tampon in for too long. Bacteria multiply, which causes infection to spread which can eventually prove fatal. Make sure you change your tampon at least once every four hours, even if you don't think it's full or if you have a light period. If you experience symptoms like high fever, confusion or nausea, go to the nearest emergency department of a hospital.

Which one to use?

It's entirely upto you. Although tampons are now available in India, some girls are reluctant to use them because they think it might break their hymen and they will no longer be a virgin. This is not true at all – a hymen has many gaps in it for your period, your urine and mucus to flow through. So when you put a tampon in, it usually just fits into one of these gaps. Also, virginity, as explained on page 109, is a word we use to describe the period before one has penetrative sex, so using a tampon has nothing to do with taking away your virginity.

Period Pangs

'Is it problematic to have your period for one month continuously?' Smita

Yes. Having a period for over a month is a sign that something is wrong. A period that lasts one month can be a sign of ovarian cysts which, if untreated, can cause problems for you later on. You are also losing a lot of blood, which will affect your energy levels. There is no reason why you should be living in such discomfort. Please go and see a doctor as soon as possible.

'My period is very light and lasts only three days. I also get a lot of smelly, yellow discharge before my period. What should I do?' Fatima

Periods can last from three days to a week so there is nothing wrong with the length of your period – as long as this is what happens each month. If your period normally lasts five days or longer and you notice a change, then visit a doctor to get yourself checked.

The fact that there is very little flow could be a sign that you are not eating enough, not exercising enough or have something stressful in your life right now. Try and eat more spinach and dal. Have a glass of milk every morning and make sure you are eating three big meals every day.

The yellow discharge that you are talking about is perfectly normal. Make sure you take a shower every day, and don't be afraid to clean your vulva properly with a mild soap. Wash out the soap thoroughly and make sure you wipe yourself completely dry afterwards. You can also wear panty liners, which are available at most chemists (if they are not available, use the thinnest pad you can find). You can change your pad every time you get discharge and this will keep you fresh.

If the discharge continues throughout the month and is always smelly, then it could be an infection like thrush, which is a yeast infection that is very common among women. It is treatable and you should visit your doctor and talk to her/him about it.

Usually, you can just take a few pills and apply an ointment near and in your vagina, and the infection will disappear within a few weeks. See Chapter 8 for more information on thrush. If you have been sexually active, discharge with an odour or colour that is different from what you normally have, might be a sign of an STD. In that case, you should seek the help of a doctor as soon as possible. See Chapter 8 for more information on STDs and how to find the right doctor for you.

'Does taking painkillers for period pains have any negative effect on the body?' Sonal

It's probably not a good idea to become dependent on painkillers every time you have your period. Once in a while, when it's particularly painful, it's acceptable to take a painkiller. If you find yourself taking a pill every day during your period, go see your doctor. In the meantime, you could try masturbating to reach orgasm – or have a look at the period pains section earlier in this chapter for other ideas on how to reduce period pains.

'What are the ways to delay the dates of your period?' Harshita

Upsetting your cycle isn't a great idea but some people find it useful if they don't want to deal with a period at a certain time – if you are going camping, for example. You can ask your doctor about starting the contraceptive pill which will allow you to control when you break for your period. But you cannot stop and start the pill so easily – doing so can be harmful. Moreover, you may also need to be on the pill for at least a month before you see any difference in your period cycle. So ask yourself why you want to delay your period. Is it worth it?

'When does your period stop?' Bonu

Your period stops when you get pregnant. For the nine months that you are pregnant, you do not have a period as the womb needs its lining and will not shed it. But once you have a baby, your period returns to normal. Generally, your period stops permanently when you approach your sixties. This is called menopause.

'Does masturbation or any other kind of sexual activity disturb one's period cycle?' Susan

Not at all. As we've mentioned earlier, masturbation can actually help relieve stomach cramps (as the orgasm relieves tension) and in no way affects your period cycle. Sex or masturbation during your period is also completely fine – it can be a little messy but it is perfectly okay and not harmful. But it's important to remember that the risk of spreading the HIV virus is higher when a woman is on her period.

Some Common Myths

You should wash your hair on the first day of your period and on the last but not in between.

You can wash your hair as much or as little as you want – your period has no bearing whatsoever on when you should wash your hair.

You cannot enter a kitchen when you have your period.

This is pretty old-fashioned. What if you need to make a cup of tea? This is one time it's really okay to break the 'rules', especially if it's a stupid, old-fashioned one.

You should not shower with soap when you have your period.

On the contrary, maintaining good hygiene is essential. You should wash every day with a mild soap, and cleaning your external genitals is essential when you have your period.

You cannot wear white clothes when you have your period.

It's probably not a great idea to wear a totally white outfit on the heaviest day of your period. But it's perfectly okay to wear white jeans, trousers, a salwar or even a white skirt when you have your period. Just change your tampon/pad frequently to avoid any embarrassing stains.

You cannot pee when you have a tampon on.

Total myth. Of course you can pee when you have a tampon on. You can poop, pee, dance, play, sit, lie down, anything you want, even if you have a tampon on.

Orgasms

'What is an orgasm? Is it normal?' Honey

An orgasm is the climax of sexual tension. It can come by having sex with someone, by masturbation or even by having a sexy dream. An orgasm is completely normal, healthy and can feel wonderful.

A Woman's Orgasm

When you are about to orgasm, your skin might feel tingly and highly sensitive to touch. Your breasts might swell and your nipples become erect. An orgasm feels like a big release after which your body significantly relaxes. Your vagina might vibrate a tiny bit as the muscles relax. A fluid is released from the urethra, but this rarely seeps out of the vagina and is definitely not urine. Orgasms can vary in the way they make you feel. Sometimes they make you feel like you are exploding with happiness, sometimes they make you feel like you just sneezed.

A Man's Orgasm

When a man orgasms, his nipples might become erect and his body tense. His penis will spurt out or ejaculate a white, thick liquid called semen, which contains thousands of sperm. A common way to describe a man's orgasm is to say 'he has come'. Ejaculation and orgasms are two separate processes but in a man, they often happen at the same time. In general, it's easier for a man to 'come' than for a woman. But there are several ways a woman can orgasm. See Chapter 6 for more information on orgasms.

Sexual Fantasies

What is a Sexual Fantasy?

Saif topless. Ranbir Kapoor in a bathtub filled with rose petals. Swimming naked with your friend. Lying down next to your boyfriend on the grass. Or dancing close to your girlfriends. All sexy scenarios, right? When we imagine ourselves in sexy situations, it is called a sexual fantasy. In some fantasies, you may have sex with someone and in some you may just kiss them or get close to them. During a sexual fantasy, we feel excited, aroused or turned on.

What Happens When We Have a Sexual Fantasy?

Your skin might feel tingly. Your nipples might become erect and hard. You might get 'wet', which is when the vagina produces a fluid to make intercourse easier and smoother. Don't expect to see liquid dripping out of you though. Getting wet is an internal process. Also, you might find that your level of lubrication varies. But this is not an indication of how aroused you are.

'Is having a wet dream or a fantasy a sign of mental illness?' Leslie

There is nothing wrong and shameful about sexual fantasies. They are a healthy, normal part of the human experience. Most of us have sexual fantasies on a regular basis so there is nothing to feel embarrassed or nervous about.

Some of us feel guilty if we have a certain type of fantasy, like wanting your friend or teacher to kiss you, for example. But it's okay to let your imagination run free. Just remember that most of the things we fantasize about are things that we would never actually want to happen in real life. There's a big difference between fantasy and reality.

During puberty and throughout your teens, your hormones are constantly in flux. This results in a heightened sense of sexuality and sex. Wet dreams and sexual fantasies are a sign of you coming to terms with who you are sexually and figuring out what you like.

'Sometimes I have sexy dreams and when I wake up, I have a discharge in my panties. What happened?' Dolly

You had what's known as a nocturnal emission or 'wet dream'. Before we have sex, the vagina prepares itself by secreting a liquid that lubricates the vaginal walls. This liquid is what you saw in your panties. You may even have reached orgasm in your sleep. This happens to most people at one point or another so it is perfectly healthy and nothing to worry about.

Masturbation

What is Masturbation?

Masturbation is when we touch ourselves to get sexually aroused. It is a common, perfectly healthy and natural part of being human. Your friends, your cousins, most of your family have at some time or the other touched their bodies and explored their sexual organs for pleasure.

Why Masturbate?

Here's what some young women had to say…

'It makes me feel sexy' Nina

'Coz it's human nature' Ritu

'It's an expression of my own sexuality, it's not harming me – or anyone else for that matter.' Anika

Maybe when your crush walked past you in the corridor today, he or she brushed your arm and made your skin tingle? Or maybe you watched a movie with an erotic scene and it turned you on? We all feel sexually buzzed and turned on from time to time and masturbation is a good way to stimulate yourself and find out what you like sexually. There is nothing shameful about touching yourself sexually. Here's what some of you had to say about masturbation:

'Having sexual desire is not bad and if someone touches herself that's her personal decision.' Nicky

'Touching yourself is the most healthy way to satisfy your sexual needs. You don't have to be with a boy and you can't get pregnant.' Sunana

'It helps you explore your body and get to know your likes and dislikes in sex.' Gurpreet

'Because if I am having fun, then why not?' Deepika

What Exactly Happens?

People usually like to be alone when they masturbate – last thing before they go to sleep or in the shower or bath. Using their hands, some people massage their breasts or their vulva. Most women rub or massage their mons pubis with their palm or by rubbing against a pillow. Some women experiment using different types of surfaces, like a towel or a soft pillow or even a cuddly toy. Others like to use a jet of water from a hand-held shower to masturbate.

Several girls like to stimulate themselves by putting their fingers or an object into their vagina. Using everyday objects like candles or carrots in your vagina is not a good idea as you can never be sure of how clean they are and what bacteria lies on their surface.

It's more than possible to reach an orgasm through masturbation. In fact, it's one of the easiest and surest ways to reach an orgasm.

Here's what some girls said about how they masturbate:

'Touching, rubbing the clitoris'

'By caressing my vagina'

'Rub their vaginas/push fingers inside themselves'

'They stroke their vagina in a fashion that gives them pleasure'

'By inserting their fingers in the vagina, sometimes by touching the clitoris as well'

Things to Remember if You are Going to Masturbate:

1. Make sure your hands are clean. Your vagina is a delicate part of your body and very susceptible to infections, like urinary tract infections (See Chapter 8 for more information on UTIs.) So, wash your hands thoroughly with soap.

2. Find a private place. You need to be relaxed if you are really going to enjoy this.

3. Only use your fingers or hands inside your vagina. It's not a good idea to put anything else in there.

4. Masturbation is a personal choice – no one is required to do it or not do it. You have to decide what works for you.

How Do Men Masturbate?

Men masturbate by using their hands to stimulate their penis. They might use one hand to hold onto their penis and then move this hand up and down on the penis until they come, or orgasm. Masturbation is pretty common among men and they might start touching themselves sexually as early as ten or eleven. There is less social taboo around men masturbating but it is still not talked about openly, even though there is nothing to feel embarrassed about. Masturbation among men is perfectly natural and healthy. It allows a man to figure out what he likes sexually, explore his body and find an outlet for his desire.

Is There Such a Thing as Too Much Masturbation?

You cannot harm your sex organs or damage your physical or mental health by masturbating, so don't worry about getting busy down there. As long as it feels good, there should be no reason to stop, worry or feel guilty.

Masturbation is as healthy as eating your vegetables. Some people do it every day, some people do it twice a day, some people once a month – it's totally up to you. But if you find yourself unable to get out of bed in the morning because you're so caught up in stimulating yourself, maybe you have gone too far! Don't give yourself a hard time though, it's probably just a phase and you'll get over it.

'I sometimes touch my breasts when I am dancing, is that considered masturbation?' Aarti

Just like washing your private parts in the shower is not considered masturbation, neither is touching your body while you're dancing. Masturbation is when we touch our private parts with the intention of sexually stimulating ourselves.

'I don't masturbate. Is there something wrong with me?' Suraya

Not at all. You might decide masturbation is not for you and there is nothing wrong with that. This does not mean you are not into sex or don't think of sexual activity as fun or enjoyable. Remember, it's your body, your choice and your life.

What Is a Vibrator?

A vibrator is a harmless sex toy that can look like a penis – they are often long and cylindrical or egg-shaped. When you put batteries in them and turn them on, they vibrate. While masturbating, women either put it on top of their clitoral hoods to stimulate the clitoris or insert it into their vaginal opening.

Sex toys are currently illegal in India so it is not recommended you use a vibrator. Not to mention, they are generally hard to find and can be costly. If you are going to use one anyway, make sure you sterilize it with soap first and follow the instructions. Don't share your vibrator with anyone.

True or False Quiz

1. Masturbation can make you go blind.
2. You can only masturbate once a day.
3. If you masturbate then you are no longer a virgin.
4. Masturbation is only for boys.
5. Everyone talks about masturbation.
6. Masturbation is a dirty thing to do.
7. You should feel guilty if you masturbate.
8. You should be gentle when you touch yourself.
9. You can get pregnant from masturbation.
10. You can masturbate even if you are in a relationship and having sex.

Answers

1. *False*. This is a myth. There is no truth in this whatsoever. Masturbation is a healthy, normal part of growing up, learning about and exploring your body.
2. *False*. You can masturbate as many times as you want to.
3. *False*. Masturbation cannot tear your hymen. Your hymen can break from playing a sport, from tampons, even from riding a bicycle when you are 14 years old! Most people consider anyone who has not had vaginal intercourse, a virgin.
4. *False*. Complete rubbish, girls. Boys masturbate regularly and so can we.
5. *False*. Strangely, even though mostly everyone has masturbated at least once in their lives, people don't talk about it much. It's hard to find someone you might trust with the information. Maybe your best friend? Has she ever tried it? But be careful who you tell. People have a way of judging and being weird even though they're up to the same thing! Typical, eh?
6. *False*. Exploring your body, learning about your sexual preferences or desires is perfectly normal. There is nothing dirty about it.
7. *False*. No, no, no. Never feel guilty about wanting to learn about your body and sexuality.
8. *True*. Touch yourself gently. Take off any sharp rings or anything that might hurt you. Go slow, move your fingers smoothly and gently. Your vagina and breasts are very delicate and should be treated with care.
9. *False*. If you are masturbating alone then you are not at risk of getting pregnant at all. If you are masturbating with someone from the opposite sex, make sure no bodily fluids come in contact with your vagina. Also, if a man is touching you after masturbating himself, make sure his hands are clean.
10. *True*. You can continue masturbating when you are in a relationship. It might even help you share with your partner how you like to be touched.

Three

Relationships

Don't forget love; it will bring all the madness you need to unfurl yourself across the universe.

Mirabai

Love does not claim possession, but gives freedom.

Rabindranath Tagore

Unlike our parents' generation, it's simpler for us to get intimate with members of the opposite sex, to become friends with a man and even to date someone without it leading to marriage. But that doesn't mean it's easy to have a boyfriend, and it certainly isn't easy for same-sex couples to date openly in India. Our romantic interests might meet with judgement from our parents, our friends and society in general. Women who date, are sexually interested in boys or other girls, or have a steady boyfriend are often labelled 'loose', 'slutty' or 'immoral'.

Some of the time it's us women who are behind the judgement of fellow women. Most of us, at some time or the other, have talked about another girl or called her a name. Maybe she broke up with someone and started dating someone else straightaway, so you called her a slut? Or maybe she went out with someone only for a day and you called her loose? Or maybe she wasn't interested in boys at all and you called her old-fashioned? We all judge each other, without even realizing it. But think about how you would feel if someone said those things about you. Is it a crime to be interested in someone? Or not be interested in anyone at all for that matter?

The minute we stop judging and start listening to one another, we might find that most women have similar anxieties. Maybe you feel torn between doing what your parents want and what you want, between going out with someone you like and not dating at all. Many of us feel embarrassed about being single. Some of us are worried that no one will find us attractive. Some of us worry that we will never find our true love. Some of us worry about our parents finding out about our partner, some worry about possessive significant others or dating someone from a different caste or community. Some feel guilty about wanting to date at all.

So even though things have changed since your parents were young, it's still difficult to know what the right thing is when it comes to the complicated world of relationships.

This chapter looks at why we feel pressured to be in a relationship in the first place. We ask questions like – *Why shouldn't we celebrate being single? Why do people make such a big deal about being in a relationship?* We explore why people are attracted to one another and give you some hints on how to flirt. We talk about developing a crush on someone and also how to let someone down gently.

The second half of this chapter focuses on the relationship itself – how to communicate well with your partner, how to resolve an argument, deal with a jealous partner, manage a long-distance relationship and handle a break-up.

Ultimately though, the most profound relationship you'll ever have is with yourself. Learning to love yourself, building on your self-esteem, respecting yourself, your body and your mind will bring you happiness that no relationship with a man or woman can ever provide.

Being Single

'All everyone talks about is relationships or boyfriends. Is having a relationship essential?' Rajni

We have all felt the pressure to be in a relationship at some point in our lives. TV shows, magazines, our friends or the Internet might lead us to believe that being in a relationship is the only route to happiness. It might even seem that, suddenly, all your friends have boyfriends. Worse, if you tell someone that you are single, you often get a response like, 'Aww, don't worry, you'll find someone soon.'

Unfortunately, there is a big misconception that being in a relationship brings you comfort, security, love and happiness. And while good, healthy relationships can indeed provide all this, so can good friends, your family or a fabulous job or hobby. Enjoying your time alone and learning to be happy sans a boyfriend/girlfriend is an essential part of becoming a healthy adult. You don't need anyone else to make you happy. Of course, knowing all this doesn't mean the pressure to date or have a boyfriend, especially when that's all your friends talk about, magically disappears! In fact, it can be pretty hard to stand your ground. But being aware of the pressure and being clear about what you want is an important step to withstanding the pressure to date. Yes, that means every time someone gives you that aww-you're-single-face, instead of wishing you could punch them, respond with a simple, 'Don't feel too sorry for me. I choose to be single and think the endless pursuit of boyfriends and relationships isn't something I am interested in.'

Of course, this is advice that applies to the younger readers out there – the ones that are just starting to date. But if you are a little older, you might find yourself under a different, more intense type of pressure. Unfortunately, there is a lot of taboo around the single woman in her twenties – she is deemed more vulnerable, more insecure, and incomplete without a man. This idea is, of course, ridiculous and laughable but societal and familial pressure can make being single in your early twenties and onwards hard. Aunties, uncles, parents, friends, siblings, community leaders, all come out of the woodwork to match you up with other men or harass you about finding someone. There is no perfect way to deal with a situation like this and you need to make a decision that makes you happy. Try talking to whoever is putting pressure on you about how you enjoy being single and why. In the meantime, stay safe, hang out with your friends, flirt with whoever you want and pursue your dreams without worrying about the strain of a full-time relationship.

'Why do I feel attracted to every handsome boy I see and want him to be my boyfriend? Am I obsessed?' Shivmeet

Having a boyfriend might seem like the most important thing in the world, especially when everyone around you seems to be in a relationship. It's perfectly normal to like guys and think about them a lot. But very few crushes lead to relationships so try not to have any expectations.

It's important to remember that being in a relationship does not guarantee happiness, intimacy or love. Try and enjoy the fact that you are single. You can flirt with whoever you want, hang out with your friends whenever you want and concentrate on your studies. That's a pretty good life, isn't it?

Friendship

'If a boy and girl are hanging out or shopping or doing anything together in a public place – why do people call them girlfriend-boyfriend and scold them?' Shruti

There is a general presumption that when a boy and girl are hanging out together, they're in a romantic relationship. Of course, this isn't always the case. Sometimes you're just friends. Either way, there's nothing to feel ashamed or guilty about.

Being friends with a boy is a healthy and normal part of being a human being.

The next time a stranger scolds you or passes a comment, ignore them. These people don't deserve your time and energy so don't let it get to you. Remind yourself that you are doing nothing wrong. If it's a parent scolding you, have a look at Chapter 5 for some tips on how to talk to your family about your life and independence.

'Is it okay to discuss "non-veg" and vulgar stuff with your cousin brothers or male friends if you are comfortable doing so? Or do boys start thinking of you as an indecent girl who is desperate to talk about all this?' Manju

'Indecent' and 'desperate' are outdated words that only serve to make a person feel like they have done something wrong. Talking, thinking about or having sex is never indecent nor a sign of desperation. In fact, it's healthy and normal to be curious about sex.

Sometimes there are nasty double standards in society which make us think that as girls, we are not supposed to think about or want sex. But if it's okay for boys to think about it, why shouldn't it be okay for us?

Discussing your feelings with your friends, whether they are boys or girls, whether it's to do with sex or the weather, is perfectly normal. Unfortunately, not everyone feels this way so make sure you trust the people you are talking to.

Crushes

'How do you know when someone is interested in you? Especially when the person is a close friend and you are afraid to risk losing the friendship.' Avni

It can be hard to turn a friendship into a relationship. It's normal to be worried that you might lose a friend if the romantic relationship doesn't work out for some reason. And this could happen...But bear in mind that some of the best relationships are based on good friendships. Take a risk and ask this person how they feel about you. If you don't feel up to doing it in person, write him/her a letter or email.

♥

FLIRTING

Flirting is when we use our body language and conversation to let someone know we are interested in him/her. There is no right or wrong way to flirt. You have to do and say what makes you feel comfortable and safe.

How do I flirt with someone?

* For centuries, women have been using their eyes and body language to let someone know they are sexually available and accessible. Smiling at someone lets them know that you are approachable.
* Turn your body to face the person you are talking to and don't cross your arms in front of you. It sends out

a message that you are defensive and have barriers up. Instead, put your hands in your pockets or behind you.

* Make eye contact.
* Listen to what they have to say and engage them in conversation.
* Flattery gets you everywhere. Pay a compliment or two during the conversation. Maybe you like his/her smile or he/she has beautiful eyes? Well, then, say so!
* Flirting is all about confidence. Truly believe you are a wonderful, beautiful person inside and outside and people will naturally gravitate towards you.

I don't want to flirt...

Some people are born flirts and some of us just find it a little silly or get too nervous when we have to talk to someone we like. Don't worry about it. You don't have to be good at flirting or even respond when someone flirts with you. Just be yourself and you are guaranteed to have a good time.

♥

'Is it okay to flirt with someone you know is interested in you but you don't like them in that way?' Ayeesha

Continuing to casually flirt with someone after you're sure they feel strongly about you and you don't feel the same about them can be really hurtful. Flirting sends out the message that you are available, interested and having fun. So the other person will continue to hope that something might happen.

The best thing to do in such a situation is to have an honest chat with the person involved. Explain to them that you are not looking for anything serious and like being single and flirting. Make it clear that you are not interested in them 'that way' but would like to remain friends. Maybe say something along the lines of, 'I really like you as a friend but I am not ready for a relationship' or 'I'm sorry but I just don't see you like that'. Tell him that you don't want this to affect your friendship. You know how wonderful he is but you're just not interested. Maybe give him a letter saying the same thing. But be sensitive.

Explain that it might be a good idea to take some space from one another so that you both have some time to get over it. Give the person some time to work through their issues. It's not going to be easy for them. Rejection is never easy – they may feel sad, angry or confused – but these feelings will subside with time.

It's natural to feel some guilt when you tell someone you're not romantically interested in them but you have nothing to feel guilty about. You cannot force yourself to like someone just because they like you, or because you feel scared or guilty about rejecting them, or because you want to be with someone just for the sake of it. Being honest, direct and clear about how you feel about someone *now* will save you and the other person a whole lot of potential heartache down the road when more feelings are involved.

In extreme cases, if you feel like your rejection might unleash some unhealthy psycho-tendencies in the other person, you may want to seek the advice of an older friend, your parents or even the police. Explain to them that you feel intimidated or threatened by this person and want to distance yourself from their romantic advances. Also, avoid meeting this person – try to let them down gently over the phone or via email. There is no easy way to do this but making sure you are always safe is very, very important.

'I get a crush on every smart and good-looking person I see. Is something wrong with me?' Sonal

Not at all! Crushes are natural and healthy. It's very normal to meet someone you like, even someone of the same sex, and develop a crush on them. When we meet people we find attractive or smart, we feel drawn to them for a few moments which is completely healthy. But these feelings are fleeting and come and go. Even though others may not talk about it, they have crushes on people just as easily.

'I had crushes on teachers of the same sex – twice. Is that okay? How far can you push, especially with a teacher...' Hemani

It's perfectly normal to have a crush on a female teacher (or a male teacher for that matter) at some point in your life. They are usually kind, dependable, sympathetic forces in our lives, so it's natural to feel some attraction towards them. But it's important to remember that it's just a crush and should not be pushed any further.

A relationship between a student and a teacher can be very problematic because of the unequal power involved. Your teacher has a lot of power and can use this influence to manipulate you into a situation you are not entirely comfortable with. You could both get into a lot of trouble if you pursue it further. Colleges and schools condemn any sexual contact between students and teachers, and you could end up getting expelled, or worse, your teacher could get fired or imprisoned if you are under the age of 16.

'I sometimes find myself getting attracted to my male friends. But I know it's not a crush or love. It's just curiosity. Will I ever be able to actually fall for someone, keeping in mind my present indecisiveness?' Binal

Having lots of crushes is perfectly healthy and normal. Some of these infatuations last weeks or months, while others only a day. You will probably meet someone that you really, really like one day. In the meantime, don't worry about liking lots of people – it's a normal part of being a young woman.

'What does it mean when you don't have a crush on anybody for a long time (say one year)?' Khadija

It doesn't mean anything really. Maybe you haven't met anyone cute or interesting in that time. Maybe you have been concentrating on your studies or spending more time with your friends. Whatever the reason, it is perfectly normal not to be sexually attracted to anyone for long periods of time. There is no right or wrong number of crushes to have or a proper way of experiencing attraction. Trust yourself and the way you feel.

What is Attraction?

Attraction is when you feel pulled or drawn towards something or someone. You could like the way someone looks, their sense of humour, their style, the kind of books they read or the way they kiss. Or maybe you can't resist their smile, their laughter, their smell. Whatever the reason, your attraction to someone can come and go in a few hours or last a lifetime.

Does He Like Me?

'How do you know when a guy is interested?' Trina

Figuring out whether a guy likes you or not is tough. They can act hot one minute, cold the next. It can drive us up the wall sometimes!

Here are some things to watch out for that could help clue you in:

- **He finds excuses to hang out with you.** Pretending he needs help with an assignment is one of the oldest tricks in the book. He just wants to spend time with you!
- **He finds reasons to touch you casually.** Maybe a graze on the arm, an arm around the shoulder, or he sits next to you when there are lots of empty seats.

- **He hangs on to your every word.** Usually, when someone is listening intently to everything you are saying, they are into you.
- **He remembers random things about you.** He knows you like lilies, that you didn't come to school last week because you had a cold, how many siblings you have.
- **He acts shy around you.**
- **He goes out of his way to make you laugh.**
- **He shows off in front of you.**

These are just little hints that he might like you. But you will never be sure until you ask him!

Do I Like Him?

He makes you laugh and you love hanging out with him at school or university, but you get nervous every time he suggests you meet each other alone. Figuring out whether you like a boy as a friend or as something more is hard.

Although there are a few general signs to watch out for – your heart skips a beat whenever he's around; you find excuses to be around him, to touch him, to sit next to him; you find yourself thinking about him constantly; you imagine what his lips might feel like – knowing whether you like someone is not something you can turn to a checklist for.

It might seem like there should be some logic to attraction and love but unfortunately, there isn't. Like when an unbelievably gorgeous boy asks you out and all your friends think you should say yes, but you're more interested in the boy who has you cracking up with laughter every time you see him. Love is a weird thing. And there are no easy answers. Only YOU can really answer the question of whether you like someone as more than a friend. Also, give it a little time. You might find that the answer will come easier with some time.

Unrequited Love

'Why does it always happen to me that the guy I like doesn't like me back. I want to date this guy – but how do I?' Lata

Are you sure he doesn't like you? How do you know for sure? Maybe you should approach him. Or tell one of your friends to find out whether he has a girlfriend. Or just ask him directly whether he likes you. You might find he's just shy and that's why he hasn't approached you yet.

If you do find that he's not interested, move on. There are plenty more fish in the sea. Take some space from him. Avoid the places you know he hangs out in and don't call or email him. A little space can work wonders. Concentrate on doing something else you enjoy, like swimming or reading to keep occupied.

As harsh as it sounds, you cannot make someone like you. And even though you might feel upset at first, it will soon pass. Don't waste your tears and time on someone who doesn't appreciate you. Chances are that someone who gets how awesome you are is around the corner.

Relationships and Sex

'Is the first step or the foundation of any relationship sex?' Radha

A lot of things go into making a relationship – attraction, compatibility, friendship and trust, to name just a few. While sex is an important and essential part of any romantic relationship, it is by no means what keeps the relationship going or what forms its foundation.

'Is it weird that I don't have any hang-ups about sex? I want to sleep with two different guys and I am not in a relationship with either of them – is there anything wrong with me?' Sita

Not at all. Not having any hang-ups about sex means you are comfortable with who you are and secure with your sexuality. Just make sure you use a latex condom each time and be honest with yourself and your partners about the fact that you aren't interested in a long-term, exclusive relationship with someone.

'Why is it that guys are always preoccupied with sex? Every time I meet my boyfriend he wants to touch me, kiss me. Even I like it but sometimes it becomes a bit too much.' Tanaz

Not all guys are preoccupied with sex! But most men develop a keen and healthy interest in sex from an early age. Their raging hormones and curiosity about women take over and they might act like they only think about sex! But the truth is, women think about sex almost as much as men do, but it's not as acceptable for them to talk about it honestly and publicly. So, it might only *seem* that men are preoccupied with sex because they are simply able to express their desire more openly.

You say that you also like it when he touches you or kisses you. So ask yourself, why do you want it to stop? Do you feel guilty or ashamed that you like it? A lot of us think we are doing something wrong by liking sex or by wanting our boyfriend to touch us. Our communities, religious leaders, families and even our friends sometimes tell us that desiring someone or letting them touch us is wrong or shameful. This can lead to years of guilt, shame and disgust at ourselves for feeling lust and desire for someone. There is, of course, nothing wrong with liking it when your lover kisses or touches you. It is a natural and healthy part of being a young woman.

Try to figure out what is bothering you. If you genuinely think he is being pushy, have an honest chat with him. Talking openly and frankly about how you feel and what you want will get you very far. And if you don't feel comfortable telling him that he needs to back off and respect your space, then maybe he's not the right man for you.

What is Intimacy?

Intimacy is when people feel incredibly close to one another. You can be intimate with your parents, your siblings, your friends and even your boyfriend/girlfriend. When you are intimate with someone, you feel comfortable around them. You usually feel a sense of familiarity and trust between you.

Communication

Communication is one of the most important aspects of a relationship. It's what most relationships are built on. We have to be able to tell our loved ones how we feel, what we like, and listen to what they have to say as well. A lot of us shy away from good communication because it often means saying things that might hurt the other person and make us unpopular for a while.

Take this quick quiz to work out how good your communication skills are.

Do you say it like it is?

1. A party's coming up. Your best friend asks if she can borrow the shoes you were planning to wear. Do you:

   a. Explain that the shoes make up an essential part of the outfit you've already picked out and suggest something else she might borrow for her getup.

b. Give them to her right away.
c. Refuse point blank and offer no explanation as to why she can't borrow them.

2. When people describe you they tend to say, she's…

a. nice and sweet.
b. tough as nails.
c. calm and strong.

3. Your boyfriend wants to hang out with his friends, but you have a romantic evening planned. Do you:

a. Throw a hissie fit until he gives in.
b. Tell him what you had planned and why it's important to you.
c. Reassure him that it's okay but fume inside.

4. Your teacher claims that you missed one of her assignments but you remember handing it in. Do you:

a. Stick to your feisty guns – you know she's wrong.
b. Compromise and re-write the assignment with an extended deadline.
c. Say nothing but vow to complain to the principal about her.

5. The cutie in your maths class asks to borrow your homework so he can copy it. Do you:

a. Hand it over and bat your eyelashes, hoping he might ask for more than just your homework.

b. Offer to help him do it instead. A little after-school time with the hottie sounds nice.
c. Politely refuse and re-think your crush on him.

6. Indian Ocean are in concert. You buy tickets for yourself and your friend Pinky. Two weeks pass, and she doesn't pay you back. Do you:

a. Never mention it. What's a little money between friends?
b. Tell her that you need the money coz you want to buy some cute jeans for the concert.
c. Borrow some money from her to even it out.

7. You sent off a great application for a magazine internship but haven't heard back yet. Do you:

a. Call the office to politely follow up on your application.
b. Presume you didn't get the internship and move on.
c. Call them, ranting and raving about what they're missing out on.

8. Your ideal job involves:

a. Constant interaction and communication, like a doctor.
b. A fearless nature and lots of confrontation, like a police officer.
c. Compassion and patience, like a nursery school teacher.

9. Your bike needs new brakes. When you go to pick it up from the repair shop, they've added new tires *and* a new seat. The total bill is way out of your budget. Do you:

a. Refuse to pay for the extra repairs – you liked your old seat and tires.
b. Negotiate a new amount for the tires and seat and congratulate yourself on your bargaining skills
c. Become nervous about a possible confrontation and pay the full amount.

Answers

1.	a) 2	b) 1	c) 3
2.	a) 1	b) 3	c) 2
3.	a) 3	b) 2	c) 1
4.	a) 3	b) 2	c) 1
5.	a) 1	b) 2	c) 3
6.	a) 1	b) 2	c) 3
7.	a) 2	b) 1	c) 3
8.	a) 2	b) 3	c) 1
9.	a) 3	b) 2	c) 1

0–9 Beat around the Bush Betty

You're a sensitive soul and don't like confrontations that make your heart race and your palms sweaty. People are drawn to your calm and sweet nature. But you like to resolve things by pretending they never happened. Speak your mind sometimes. Raising your voice about your feelings is healthy. When that voice inside tells you to say 'no', go with it.

10–18 Delightfully Direct

Communication is your middle name. You're assertive and articulate in expressing your needs. When faced with sticky situations and disagreements, you seek to explain your opinions carefully and clearly without offending anyone. But remember, it's natural to lose your cool sometimes. And at other times silence is golden.

19–27 Confrontational Communicator

Woah there, girl! You're not afraid to speak your mind and never let people get the better of you. You are strong-willed and fear doesn't feature in your personality. But listening to what another person has to say will take you a long way. Don't be so quick to take on a fight.

When You're in a Relationship

Trust

'How do you know if your boyfriend is serious about you?' Lourdes

This is a toughie. It's hard to ever know for certain whether someone is serious about you. But here are some general tips that might help you decide if your boyfriend is committed and trustworthy:

- How long have you been together? If you've been together for a reasonable amount of time – let's say six months – chances are that he's serious about you.

- Has he reassured you? If so, the fact that your boyfriend has taken the time to remind you how much he loves and cares for you means he is serious about making you feel treasured and comfortable.
- Has he introduced you to his friends? If he wants you to meet his pals, it means that he is ready to make the relationship public. If he's willing to involve his friends or family, there's every indication that he's into you.

Remember, these are just general guidelines. Only you will be able to figure out whether or not you can trust your partner. Listen to yourself and trust your judgement.

Arguing

'I have been in a relationship for a year and a half but we fight a lot. My boyfriend is extremely short-tempered. Help!' Ayeesha

Does your boyfriend get angry over little things or without any warning? If you answered yes to this question, then you might need to take a break from this guy. People who lose their temper for no apparent reason usually have something going on in their lives or in their past that has made them a very angry person. They have issues that need to be resolved. Tell him you feel hurt by his anger and give him some space. Sometimes people need to work through their problems on their own and no matter how much we love them, we cannot do much to help.

Constantly arguing in a relationship can be very suffocating and really stunt your growth as a person. Some people will continue to throw tantrums, sulk over little things or lose their temper as long as we let them. This type of behaviour borders on being emotionally abusive at times. But your life doesn't have to revolve around someone else's mood swings. Don't let your irritable boyfriend rob you of the fun stuff in life, like having a relaxed, good time with your friends.

Jealousy

'I am in a relationship with someone but he still looks at other girls. What should I do?' Lucky

It's perfectly natural for people in a committed relationship to still be attracted to other men and women. I'm sure you occasionally look at other guys and think they're cute, right? It doesn't mean you are any less committed or attracted to your boyfriend. The same could be true of him.

On the other hand, if you think your boyfriend's eyes are wandering too far, confront him. Tell him it hurts you when he looks at other girls and ignores you. Ask him how he would feel if you were flirting with other guys. Maybe you'll find that he respects your feelings enough to stop paying attention to other girls. But keep in mind that he might also ignore your worries and change nothing about his behaviour. If this is the case, ask yourself whether you really want to be with someone who completely disregards your concerns. Can you really trust someone like that? Do you trust him enough to behave the same when you're not around? If the answer is no, reassess your relationship and figure out whether it's worth the heartache.

Lastly, jealousy can often stem from poor self-esteem. So ask yourself if you feel confident and happy right now. If not, maybe work on your self-esteem and see if the situation improves. Chapter 1 has some useful tips on building self-esteem.

Cyber Dating

'Is cyber dating okay? I have never met the person I am talking to online but I think he is genuinely interested in me.' Renuka

With all the technology we have nowadays, like email, webcams, mobiles and chatrooms, it's easy to meet and get to know people who are far away. While there is nothing wrong with long-distance relationships, it's better to meet someone first, establish the relationship and then if one of you moves away, keep it going. Why commit yourself to someone who is miles away and whom you have never met? How do you know whether you are physically attracted to him or not? You might be missing out on a relationship with someone who is much closer.

If after chatting with someone and exchanging emails, you feel like you are ready to meet in person, please take a few precautions. Cyber dating is fine but requires extra attention to safety because of the anonymous nature of the Internet. In other words, it's hard to know whether someone is being honest about who they are. So make sure you pick a public place to meet and only arrange to meet in the daytime. Take a friend with you. The Internet is crawling with pranksters, molesters and dangerous people. No matter how well you think you know him or even if you feel like you love him, *don't take any risks* and *never* go to his house or his friend's place. Never give out your personal details either, like your address or your school/ university's name.

Unfortunately, like any relationship with any person, there are no guarantees. You might end up meeting the love of your life online and then again, you might meet the biggest psycho on the planet. As always, trust your instincts. But exercise greater caution with cyber dating. Give yourself time and always protect yourself. Playing it safe and taking it slow are extremely important.

'Is it okay if I send my boyfriend sexy pictures or videos of myself through email or the Internet? Will that affect our relationship in any way?' Shruti

The best way to make any relationship last is good communication and honesty. Listening to each other and being honest about how you feel is very important. And remember that it's not just up to you, as the woman, to make things work. It always takes two people – you *both* have to be committed and work hard at the relationship.

Distance can often lead to fights, miscommunication and jealousy. But communicating well with your boyfriend and continuing to give time to the other things in your life – like your school, friends and family – will not only help you remain independent and strong as an individual but also keep your relationship healthy and happy.

About the sexy pictures, you have to ask yourself this – do you trust him 100 per cent? How long have you known each other? Because the last thing you want is for your picture to end up in the wrong hands. Think about how you might feel if someone else saw it, or if he showed it to one of his friends. And even if you trust him, what if he loses it or someone steals it? If you answer these questions honestly and still decide you want to send one, then please be careful. Make sure you get one of your trusted girlfriends to take the picture or take it yourself. Also, why not ask him for a sexy picture also? That way it's an exchange and you'll have something to look at too.

Sharing a sexy picture may not necessarily change the relationship if it is done in the right way. But if you do send him a picture and he shares it or loses it, you may lose your trust in him and that will change the relationship. You might also feel an increased sense of vulnerability after sharing something so private.

There are many other, safer ways you can explore each other sexually over long distances. Tell him about your fantasies over the phone. Or let him know what kind of underwear you're wearing that day.

Long-distance Relationships

'My guy's studying in a different state, we get to speak just once a month but whenever we speak, it feels the same. We like each other but somehow we never say it. How do I deal with the relationship?' Rajni

Ask yourself what you want from this relationship. If you do want to pursue this relationship romantically, make it clear that you are interested in taking it to the next level. Don't wait for him to say something, *you* say something! It doesn't have to be 'I love you'. It can be something like, 'What would you call our relationship?' Or say something like, 'I miss you and think about you a lot. Do you think about me?' What have you got to lose? If he responds in a way that makes you feel good, maybe the relationship is worth it despite the distance. Otherwise, it's time to seriously wonder whether you have a future together.

Cheating

'What do you do if someone you loved cheated on you? I really regret loving him.' Smiti

Cheating is a hard thing to understand. Being cheated on can leave you feeling sad, confused, insecure and angry. At a time like this, you need to remember three important things. Firstly, these feelings are temporary. With a little time and distance, you will move on, and probably realize that you're better off without this person.

Secondly, it's very easy to be vulnerable and to wonder what you did wrong, what you said to 'make him leave'. But take a deep breath and realize that the cheating had absolutely nothing to do with you. People cheat for a myriad reasons but none of these reasons has anything to do with who you are.

Lastly, try not to rush into another relationship straight away, however tempting it might be to have a new lover. Instead, take this time to be really good to yourself. Spend time with friends and family, read, watch movies, go shopping, exercise, do all the things you enjoy.

Four

YOU AND YOUR FAMILY

We are heavily influenced by our parents and family in the way we think about sex, relationships and ourselves. For example, if our parents gossip about someone they know who has married out of caste or community, it sends a subtle message to us that anything that goes against tradition is wrong. Or if our parents sleep in separate rooms, it might give us the impression that sex is wrong and something to be embarrassed about. Sometimes the messages are less subtle – maybe you have been told that you cannot have any guy friends, or that you will only be allowed to marry the boy your parents choose. Maybe your parents have implied that sex is only something that happens after marriage, and even then, only to have kids, not for pleasure.

It can be really difficult to suddenly discover that you don't feel the same way as your family about things like boys, girls, relationships, sex or your body; that the people whom you have always trusted and respected suddenly don't understand you or what you want. This happens to most of us. Once we become adults, we feel quite differently towards our parents. Maybe we don't think premarital kissing, flirting or sex is such a big deal or that there's anything wrong with same-sex relationships or love marriages. While these realizations can be unsettling, they just mean that you're forging your own individual adult identity, which is a very normal, healthy and inevitable part of growing up. You are figuring out what you think of the world and the space you would like to occupy in it.

Unfortunately, trying to explain this to your parents and family can be incredibly hard. No parent finds it easy to believe that their little girl is all grown up, and worse, doesn't share their values. In the next few pages, you will find suggestions on how to talk to your parents and how to discuss your life with them. We will try to help you communicate more effectively with your family.

Dealing with your family is never going to be easy, but it's about finding a balance between doing what you want and listening to what your parents want for you. Sometimes, after good communication, parents might realize that they have to change with the times and be more accommodating to their daughters as they turn into women.

But sometimes you might hit a wall. Sometimes our families may not be open to listening or changing their views. In this case, only you can decide the right way to think and act. In extreme cases, you might have to choose between your family and security and your independence and convictions, and these choices are the toughest ones in life. In this chapter, you will find some advice on how to deal with these heart-wrenching decisions – how to make compromises between what we want for ourselves and what others want for us.

Once again, trust, respect and listen to yourself and you might find the answer will come quicker than you expected.

No Freedom

'My parents don't allow me to go anywhere with friends and they would freak out if they ever caught me talking to a guy. They are very conservative and say that I am innocent and too young to understand the ways of the world. How can I make them give me more freedom and trust me and see me as a grown up?' Bansri

Your parents grew up in a different world in which there were no coffee shops, cinema complexes or malls. Their parents were probably really strict and in those days most kids did what they were told to. So it's only natural that your parents are going to find it difficult to come to terms with you wanting to socialize, hang out with your friends or even talk to a guy.

But it's not as hopeless as it sounds. Your parents are probably just worried about you and are having a hard time showing their concern in a way that isn't yelling or freaking out. So why don't you take the first step and let them know how you feel, that you find their rules claustrophobic and conservative. Show them that you are a trustworthy, mature young woman, and they are bound to back off a little. Here are some tips that might come in handy if you choose to do this:

- Be as open as possible when talking about your life. If you are secretive, your parents might feel like you are hiding something from them. You don't have to include all the details but you can tell them a little bit about yourself – like what kind of music you like, where you like to eat, what your friends' names are.
- Stick to the curfews and rules for a while. Prove to them that you can be trusted. If they tell you to come home by ten, then make sure you're home by half past nine.
- Cover all the bases. If they allow you to go out, give them your friends' mobile numbers and their addresses. If they think they know where you are the whole night, they may be less worried.
- Invite your friends over to your place a couple of times. Introduce your parents to your friends, and they will see how nice and trustworthy they are.
- Persist! Explain to your parents over and over again that going out with people your own age is healthy. You are not doing anything wrong.

Sharing Your Life with Your Family

'My mum says that whenever I start dating, she is fine with it as long as she knows about it. But then she judges my friends for being in relationships. How can I tell her about my boyfriend?' Abha

Sit down with her one day or offer to go shopping with her and talk to her. Ask her why she thinks your friends are doing something wrong by having a boyfriend or what it is that she doesn't like about their boyfriends. Tell her how her judgement makes you feel afraid to be honest with her, and makes you apprehensive about the future. If she was open and honest with you in the beginning – enough to realize that you may want a boyfriend some day – then you owe her the same honesty now.

Marriage

'If a woman isn't married, is she seen as bad in the eyes of society?' Ishita

This is a difficult question that everyone has to answer for themselves. Even though a lot of emphasis is placed on marriage in India, getting hitched is not necessary and you may decide it's not for you.

Deciding to live life according to your rules and not your parents' or society's is not going to be easy. And you may have to fight for what you want. So you need to ask yourself what will make you happier – pleasing yourself or conforming to the values of others. There's no easy answer to this question.

Good communication can take you far in tough situations like this. Keep in touch with what you want, have the confidence and faith that you know what's best for you, and try to calmly and honestly communicate this to those around you. The only way anything can change is if more of us talk about what we want, support one another and have confidence in our decisions.

'Why is a girl's marriage such an issue in families?' Mumtaz

It goes without saying that there is a major gender bias when it comes to girls and marriage. Parents often feel that a single daughter is vulnerable and can be the target of abuse. Or they might feel that once a daughter is married, she is no longer their financial or emotional responsibility. Whatever the reason, having your parents obsess about the man you are going to marry can drive you crazy.

The only rational way around this is to talk to your parents about what you want. Do you want to get married? If so, do you want to choose your partner yourself or are you happy to marry the boy they choose for you? Figure out what you want and try and communicate this to your family. Running away or freaking out isn't going to get you very far. Handle the situation maturely. Even though it might not seem like it right now, your parents do love you and want what's best for you. So they may be willing to listen to what you have to say.

Going against the norm is never going to be easy, so be ready to fight for what you want and piss off your parents in the process. But do it one day at a time and you may gain some ground, bringing you closer to what you want. You will find some tips on how to talk to your parents later in this chapter.

'Can women manage careers and post-wedding homes with equal success?' Lata

I know thousands of women who work full time and manage households. But why should they have to do both? If your husband works, is he expected to come home and make dinner? Or do the laundry? Nope. So why should you be expected to do both? It makes sense to share household responsibilities. That way it's easier on both working individuals.

If your family, your husband's family or your husband is giving you a hard time about working after marriage, don't let it get to you. Explain to them that you are able to do both, and that for you, it is essential to be fulfilled both at home and in your career. Although it might be hard at first, a little persistence can go a long way and you might find they will make a compromise eventually.

Finally, have faith in yourself that you know what you want and what's best for you. If you have confidence in yourself and in your decisions, people tend to back off after a while. Working after marriage will help you maintain your independence and keep you connected with your colleagues and friends. Research shows that having a stimulating, rewarding experience outside the home can work wonders in terms of building your self-esteem.

If you decide you don't want to work after marriage, that's perfectly fine too, of course. Some of us want to pour all our energies into other parts of our lives, like our family, home or social life.

Live by your own rules, whatever those might be.

Convincing Your Parents You Know What You Want

'How do you convince your parents of a guy, when your parents have had a love marriage and theirs is not working out properly?' Chitra

It might be hard to believe, but your parents were once young and will probably understand how you're feeling. The fact that their marriage is not working right now has nothing to do with whether they had a love marriage or an arranged marriage – sometimes marriages just don't work out.

The best thing to do is to talk to your parents. Show them you are adult enough to make your own decisions, prove how intelligent and level-headed you are and that you are serious about this boy. Remind them how they felt about one another when they first met.

TALKING TO YOUR PARENTS

'I sincerely wish my parents were a bit more open about stuff like sex!' Dimple

- Approach your parents when they are in a relaxed mood, not when they are trying to get ready for work or when there are guests in the house.

- Try not to be defensive or expect the worst. Chill out and give them a chance to talk.
- Bring up a general topic like dating. Ask them what they think of it. This will allow you to test the waters and see whether your parents would be open to you dating.
- Ask them how they met. Was it a love marriage or an arranged marriage? When did they know that they loved one another? How do they feel about love marriages?
- If they ask you questions, be as honest as possible.
- Open up about your life one day at a time. Share a few details about where you hang out or who your friends are.
- Try speaking to your sister, cousin or whoever you feel closest to. Ask them their advice about how to approach your parents or ask them to come with you when you talk to your parents.
- Remember that you don't have to agree with everything your parents say. It's okay to have your own opinions.
- Don't let anyone guilt-trip or manipulate you into a corner. Parents can sometimes pull the whole 'If you loved me, you would do as I say…' Just make healthy, informed decisions that make you feel proud of who you are and you'll be more than fine.
- You may need to be selective in what you tell your parents. For example, you can tell them that a group of girls are going to the cinema and that some boys might be there. You will be home by 11 p.m. and will have your mobile on you the whole time. You don't have to tell them that at the movie, you and your boyfriend may kiss.
- Some parents might threaten to take you out of college or marry you off because they are worried that you are seeing someone. Unfortunately, in this case you may have to be a little secretive. But you must be responsible and never put yourself in any risk, like getting into a car with

boys you hardly know or coming home alone when it's late at night, you have nothing to worry about.
- If you think your parents are receptive, offer to introduce your boyfriend to them. Tell them about all the wonderful things about him – what he is studying or how well he treats you or how smart he is.
- Be patient. Remember that real change doesn't happen overnight. But slowly things will probably get better.

Living Life by Your own Rules

'Is dating someone without informing your parents, cheating them? How is lying to them about going out and stuff wrong?' Leila

This is a really tough question that I get a lot. Often, girls are not expected to date before marriage. So, approaching your parents about your love life can be tricky. They can be over-protective because they're worried about your future or what their community will say. There are those of you who come from very strict families where dating or any type of romance before marriage is completely out of the question. And if your parents ever found out, you would be in big, big trouble. If this is you, then you need to weigh the positives and negatives of telling your parents about your love life. Most young women told me they wished they could confide in their parents and ask them questions about sex and relationships. Unfortunately, this isn't always possible. Your parents had a lot less freedom in their lifetime, so they might find it hard to understand why you want the things you do.

If you do decide to lie, you need to ask yourself some serious questions. How do you feel about lying to them? Are you ready to deal with the consequences if they find out? Can you look after yourself? Do you know how to be safe? Only once you're sure you know the answers to these questions, are you ready to handle the responsibility that comes with living life according to your own rules.

'My father wants me to marry a boy from my caste, but the guy I am falling for is not from the same caste.' Namita

Wanting to choose your own husband is healthy and normal, and it's okay to demand this for yourself. Unfortunately, your family may not see it this way and might force you to choose between them and making your own decisions. If you go your own way, you could have a successful, happy, healthy life but you stand to lose your family and community. It's a tough decision and one that only you can make – remember that there are no guarantees in life and neither decision ensures happiness.

Unfortunately, your family and community can also revert to violence to stop you from marrying someone they do not approve of. If you feel in danger, you should confide in someone you trust and who you think might be able to help you, like a professor at your college or your doctor.

Five | SEXUAL ORIENTATION

Figuring out who you are and what you like is a lifelong process. Similarly, realizing that you are attracted to people of the same sex, or gay, is a process that can take months, years, even a lifetime. From the day we were born, many of us were told fairytales about a prince and a princess, shown movies about heroes and heroines, and convinced that we would fall in love with someone of the opposite sex. So, when you discover that you are attracted to someone of the same sex, it's only natural to feel lonely, worried or think there is something wrong with you.

But exploring the possibility that you might be gay, bisexual or transgender is an important step to living a more open and liberating life. In this chapter you will find answers to questions like *How do I know I am gay?* and *Where can I find other gay people?* We also have a comprehensive guide to 'coming out' – advice on how to tell your family and friends that you are gay.

This chapter is mainly for women who are attracted to other women. But this chapter is *also* for women who are attracted to men. Why? Because in the next few pages, you will also find advice on how to listen sensitively if a friend or family member tells you they're gay; how to overcome homophobia – a fear of the gay community; and a quiz on stereotypes that guarantees to challenge even the most open-minded of us.

What Does Sexual Orientation Mean?

Sexual orientation is a term used to describe your sexual preferences. A man who is sexually attracted only to other men is described as **gay** or **homosexual**. A woman who is sexually attracted only to other women is called a **lesbian** or **homosexual**. A man or woman who is sexually attracted to people of both sexes is **bisexual**. A woman who is sexually attracted only to men or a man who is sexually attracted only to women is described as **straight** or **heterosexual**.

How Do I Know if I am a Lesbian?

'How is one sure if they are straight or gay?' Pooja

Monica Mody, queer activist and lawyer, says: If we lived in another time, perhaps it would not have been necessary for you to ask this question. You could 'be straight' or you could 'be gay', depending on how you felt at the moment, and either would have been okay. After all, desire keeps on changing: some people desire only men; others desire only women; others desire both men and women – which is why it is so confusing when we have to choose, when we have to put a label on ourselves and our desires.

The fact that you are questioning your sexuality means that you are probably not entirely heterosexual. Unfortunately, there are no tests for finding out if we are gay, straight or bisexual. The only thing we can go by is our feelings about other people: those of our gender and those of the opposite gender. Sometimes we know, right from the beginning, whom we're attracted to. And sometimes we are confused and need to spend time with different people to figure out what we want.

There is no hurry. Ask yourself: Am I sexually aroused by thinking about touching women, or men? If it's consistently women, then give yourself time to explore, to experience different relationships and interactions. Find out what is pleasurable for you. Don't be afraid of your feelings: your sexuality is an integral part of who you are and owning it will help you live a life truer to yourself.

Nikita began an email dialogue with me about the confusion she felt around her sexuality. Here is a short extract:

Dear Anjali,

I have been thinking about my sexuality. First of all, it's just a fact of life that I have been more attracted to women in my life than to men. I rarely get that passionate about men the way I do about women... perhaps never.

What I want to ask you is – how do I know? It might sound like a basic fact but I don't know this basic fact about myself. Maybe I get an inferiority complex when I see other girls having boyfriends when I, at some level, don't share or even understand this whole concept.

Thanks, Nikita

Dear Nikita,

Exploring your sexuality and attraction for others is a healthy and normal part of growing up, and a great first step to discovering who you are and what you like. However, there's no 'checklist' you can tick off, no 'list of questions' you can answer to determine whether you are gay or not. Sexuality is an intrinsic part of who you are and you usually just know whether you are gay or straight or bisexual or transgender.

Having said that, there are some signs you could watch out for to get a better sense of your sexual orientation. For example, the very fact that you are starting to ask some questions about your attraction to the same sex is an indication that you might feel like you are gay. Also, if you find yourself repeatedly drawn and attracted to women, you might see this as a sign that you prefer women to men. Do you masturbate? If you do, then who do you think about? When you fantasize, who do you think about? If the answer is women, then chances are that you are attracted to women.

Remember that it's okay not to be sure, and to take your time to figure out what you like and want sexually. No two people like or want the same thing and we all feel confused about our sexual preferences around this age. You do not need to have any clear answers right now. Not being able to identify with your friends when they talk about having boyfriends can be hard and make you feel lonely. But this is a temporary feeling – we all feel alienated and isolated from our friends at some point during our lives. As you grow more comfortable with who you are, it will be easier to be yourself around your friends and seek out new, more like-minded friends.

Coming to terms with your sexual orientation is a long, difficult process but reaps the wonderful reward of living a life that is true and honest to you. Feeling attracted to members of the same sex is as natural and beautiful as feeling attracted to someone of the opposite sex. What you feel is perfectly normal and shared by millions of people around the world.

What Does Bi-curious Mean?

Monica Mody says: If you have a heterosexual encounter, that does not make you straight; if you have a homosexual encounter, that does not make you gay. In fact, there's even a term 'bi-curious', for people who are curious about sexual encounters with people they are not primarily attracted to, or if they have an equal preference for men and women.

With time, you will know if you want to give a label to your feelings. Be kind to yourself as you are coming to terms with this, and remember, whether you are straight or gay does not make you any less or more normal as a person.

What Do I Do if I Think I Am Gay?

Joining a local gay and lesbian support group is a great place to start. This is a safe space where like-minded, sensitive people share their stories and advice. The resources section at the end of this book will give you a list of support groups in your area.

You might also want to confide in someone you trust. The term 'coming out' is used to describe the process of being more open about our sexual preferences with the important people in our lives.

Monica Mody with Some Advice on Coming Out

It's important to remember that you don't have to come out to anybody unless you are completely comfortable. You do not owe it to anyone to be open about your sexuality unless you want to. The rule of thumb is to *feel ready* when you come out. Since you cannot control how people are going to react, you should take what steps you can to feel prepared to handle whatever happens after you come out.

- In the beginning, think carefully and select certain people to talk to, whom you know from experience to be sympathetic and non-judgemental. If you know other gay people, you may want to come out to them first. But even then, bear in mind that people will have different reactions to your coming out. Some might be happy for you; some might disapprove. Prepare yourself mentally for any reaction.

- Test the waters. Start a discussion about a gay character/theme in a recent movie or a gay-related issue in the news and see how they react. But don't take any reactions to heart – remember that your family members love you and could feel very differently when it comes to you.
- You don't have to launch into a long explanation at first. Drop a casual remark about your weekend date with her into the conversation.
- If you are nervous about talking, put everything down in a letter and give it to your mother or father. Make it clear that you are there to answer any questions.
- Find out as much as you can about being gay. Expect people you come out to, to have lots of questions. Arm yourself with the knowledge you need. See the resources chapter at the end of this book for more information.
- If there is a queer group or queer support group in your area, get in touch with them or at least keep their contact information handy.
- Give your loved ones time to get used to it. You might find that your family doesn't accept your queerness or chooses to ignore the fact that you have come out to them. This can be extremely painful. But continue to believe in yourself. Unfortunately, we are often taught to have little tolerance for those who are different from us. The difference could

be caste, class, region, religion, or it could be sexuality. The point is to remember to celebrate ourselves and our differences.

What Do I Do if My Friend/Cousin/Sister/Brother Tells Me They Are Gay?

Try and be as sensitive and caring as possible. Here are a few suggestions on how to handle the situation.

- Listen to your friend or sister or brother carefully. Don't interrupt, let them finish talking.
- Try not to react straightaway. Remember that this person is going through a difficult time right now and has mustered up a lot of courage to talk to you, so value their trust.
- Remember that they're still the same person; nothing has changed about their personality or what they mean to you.
- If a female friend tells you that she's gay, don't presume she's attracted to you. This is one of the most common presumptions but rarely ever true – your friend isn't attracted to every single girl, just like you aren't attracted to every single boy.
- Reassure them that you understand what they are saying and that you still love them.
- If you find that you are not comfortable with what's happening, explain to your friend or sibling that you need some time to digest what he or she has just told you. See how you feel in a few days – you might realize that it's no big deal.

Being Gay in India

Same-sex relationships have now been decriminalized in India. This is a huge feat for all the activists who worked hard to change the regressive law that criminalized homosexuality in India. As a member of the gay community in India, you now have the right to maintain a relationship with someone of the same sex, attend a gay bar and read gay literature. Society, though, can be slow to catch up to the new, much-needed changes in the law, so don't expect everyone to be happy about the decision. What's most important now is that you have the legal right to be who you are.

Homophobia

Homophobia is when people are prejudiced against gay, lesbian or bisexual communities. Like any other prejudice, homophobia is horrible and can make another person feel scared, lonely and hurt. Some gay and lesbian people get beaten up by the police or by strangers. Some get threatened, some get teased, some get turned away from jobs, some aren't allowed to rent a house, some are ignored.

Do you think any of this is acceptable? Don't we all have the right to be who we are and make decisions for ourselves? Is it okay to make a person feel miserable just because of their sexual orientation? How would you feel if someone ignored or made fun of you or, worse, beat you up just because of how much money your dad made? Or because of what caste you are from? Or just because you're a girl?

If you are at the receiving end of this type of harassment, then take a deep breath and realize that their teasing and abuse has nothing to do with you. It has everything to do with them. Bullies usually pick on someone else because they want to divert attention away from themselves. They have something to hide. Join a support group and talk to them about how you are feeling. You may find that a lot of people have experienced what you are going through and can offer some advice on what to do to make it better. See the resources chapter for a list of organizations you might reach out to.

If you are someone who teases other people and makes them feel bad about who they are, take a good look at yourself. What if you found out your best friend or brother was gay? Would you want someone to treat them like that?

There are several theories that state that homophobia stems from having gay or lesbian tendencies that have been suppressed. People are often scared by what they feel towards members of the same sex and lash out at other people in order to prove to the rest of the world how straight they are.

True or False Quiz

Are you as open-minded as you think? This quiz promises to challenge some of the misconceptions held about the gay community. Read on…

1. All gays are child molesters
2. Lesbians don't have proper sex
3. If you are gay, you are just looking for attention
4. Being gay is unnatural
5. Homosexuality can be cured
6. Homosexuality is contagious
7. Gay sex is disgusting

8. AIDS is a gay disease
9. You can tell someone is gay just by looking at them

Answers

1. *False*. This is one of the biggest myths floating around. In fact, statistics and research prove the opposite is true. One study reported that 90 per cent of sexual abuse cases are committed by straight or heterosexual men.
2. *False*. Ask yourself, what is 'proper' sex? Is it feeling close to someone, getting aroused by them and enjoying an intimacy with them? Do you really need penises for that? It is very possible to orgasm from oral sex or simply by rubbing the clitoris, so lesbians can enjoy as healthy and satisfying a sex life as anyone else. Penetrative sex is the primary way to conceive, and many people consider this the only way to have 'proper' sex. But sex is also about feeling intimate and close with another person, irrespective of their gender.
3. *False*. Declaring your sexual orientation has nothing to do with looking for attention. Coming out is a very brave and difficult thing to do. No one takes this decision lightly so if someone tells you they are gay, be sensitive and don't accuse them of looking for attention.
4. *False*. Being gay is as natural as being straight. Research shows that homosexuality is genetic and pre-determined, just like eye colour or right-handedness. In other words, your sexuality, whether you are gay or straight, is as natural as all the other things you were born with!
5. *False*. Some people think they can convince gay people to become straight. Being gay is something that comes from within and cannot be 'cured' or changed. Nor should anyone try to change it. It's like saying, having a sense of humour can be cured. Your straightness

is a quintessential part of who you are and it cannot be changed, right? Same with being gay or a lesbian. It is just who you are.

6. *False*. Homosexuality is not contagious. It is not a disease or a condition so it cannot be 'caught'. It is something that comes from within and no one can be convinced to change their sexual orientation or catch it from someone else.
7. *False*. Gay people and lesbians have sex much the same way as straight people do. A lot of straight couples engage in oral sex and/or anal sex which we do not find disgusting. Some same sex couples just touch one another or engage in oral sex without any penetration. Why should this be disgusting to anyone?
8. *False*. This is another myth. In the United States, when AIDS was first noticed, it mainly affected the gay community and so it came to be labelled as a 'gay disease'. But since then HIV has largely become a disease not restricted to any sexual group – it affects anyone who is engaged in unprotected sexual activity, regardless of their sexual orientation, caste, community or country.
9. *False*. You cannot tell if someone is gay by looking at them. Just like you cannot tell whether someone is smart or stupid by looking at them. Many people have the idea that a gay man is feminine and acts like a woman and that a lesbian is more masculine and into things like sports. These are unfair stereotypes and while it is sometimes true that a lesbian can be masculine, so can a straight girl. Do you think all girls that play sports are lesbians? If you play a sport does it mean you are a lesbian or make you more masculine?

Six

SEX

When most people think of sex, they think of a man and a woman. They imagine a penis penetrating a vagina. But sex is so much more. It's not just about penetrative sex, but about a whole range of activities, feelings and sensations that may exist between a man and a woman or between two women or two men.

What does sex mean to you? Some of us consider kissing or touching one another with clothes on as sex. For some people, putting your mouth on someone's body or letting them kiss you on your genitals constitutes sex. Some of us think only sexual activity that leads to orgasm is real sex. Some people think having a fantasy and masturbating is sex. In other words, sex means different things to different people.

But there is one thing we can all agree on. Sex is a complicated matter. It can give you a lot of pleasure, allow you to explore your body and feelings and be an exciting adventure. At the same time, it can also make you feel vulnerable, used or guilty. And for that reason, it's a good idea to be completely ready before you have sex with someone. In this chapter, you will find some useful advice to help you figure out whether you are prepared to launch into Planet Sex. We offer a few suggestions on issues you might want to think about and questions you might want to ask yourself like: *Do you trust the person you want to sleep with? Are they willing to use a condom? Do you feel sexually attracted to them?*

Whether or not to have sex for the first time with someone is a decision only you can make. But it's important to remember that the **legal age** for sex in India is 16 for heterosexual sex (a woman and a man) and 18 for homosexual sex (a woman and a woman or a man and a man). Also, understanding the physical risks of sex is essential before you can grapple with the emotional and psychological aspects of sex. You should first read Chapters 7 and 8, which provide details on protecting yourself from STDs and pregnancy, before embarking on any sexual activity.

The second half of this chapter outlines the main types of sexual activity. Those of us who are new to sex (and even those who are not) probably have lots of questions. Here, we give you the basic facts about what happens, what goes where and what you might feel at the time. You might find that you can have a great time without ever having penetrative sex (although that can be fun too).

Remember that almost everybody, both men and women, experiences anxiety over the act of sex. We all worry whether we did something right or whether we made the right noises or whether we should have done more (or done less). We all feel crushed if our partner isn't adequately aroused or if he or she is overexcited. That's why at the end of the sexual activity section, you will find a Q&A which aims to answer all your questions about sex, including: *How can you tell whether a guy really loves you during sex? Will my vagina become loose after sex? My boyfriend reaches orgasm almost immediately after we start having sex, what's going on?*

Virginity

'Does a girl lose her virginity if she has allowed a man to kiss her/touch her breasts/feel her all over?' Sangeeta

Technically, a virgin is someone who hasn't had sex yet. Sex is defined as penetrative intercourse, which means a penis has entered a vagina. So, if you have given someone a blow job, they have touched you, or you have kissed, you are described as sexually active but technically still a virgin.

But virginity is really an idea or mindset and it is up to you to decide how much importance you want to give it. There is a lot of emphasis on virginity in the world. Some people believe that you should abstain from sex until your wedding night. Other people think that experimenting with your sexuality before marriage is an essential part of being a healthy adult. There is no right or wrong way to view virginity. Ultimately, you have to do what feels right to you.

Your Partner's Virginity

Discovering that your partner is not a virgin might initially scare or intimidate you. But instead of getting upset and judging them, think about the fact that they were honest with you. It is an indication that they want to start the relationship on a healthy, honest note. They want to put the past behind them. Let them. Put it behind you too, and move on.

If you find that your partner is a virgin on your wedding night and you're not, you could:

1. Be truthful and face the consequences. Many men, unfortunately, can have double standards about this sort of thing. They expect you to stay a virgin but have no such rules for themselves. Most men, while initially disappointed, will get over it and love you no matter what. Reassure him during this period – make him feel treasured and loved.
2. Lie and say you are – no one can tell if you are a virgin or not, even by using a magnifying lens. But would you really want to start off your relationship on an untruthful note? A happy relationship is based on good communication, trust and friendship among other things. So lying about your virginity means you will have to hide a little of who you are from this new man in your life. But if you feel he will react badly and the consequences will be major, then maybe spare him the details.

Your Hymen

'What if you don't bleed after having sex for the first time? What will he think?' Fawzia

The dictionary defines hymen as 'a fold of mucous membrane partly closing the external orifice of the vagina in a virgin', which basically means that there is a thin layer covering your vaginal opening. It is traditionally believed that when a woman has sex for the first time, she will bleed because her hymen tears.

In reality, the hymen means nothing and is no indication of whether you have had sex. Some women are born with no hymen or with an incomplete hymen, some women's hymens stretch during puberty and become very elastic, some hymens tear during gymnastics or regular exercise like riding a bike, and some hymens are so stretchy that they do not even tear during sex. Relating sex with the hymen is a very old-fashioned idea. Besides, no one can see your hymen or check whether it is torn just by looking at you.

'When is the right time to lose my virginity?' Sameera

Is there such a thing as the 'right time'? Everyone expects something different from having sex for the first time. Some people think it has to be romantic, some think it has to be passionate, some of us are in a hurry to get it over with. In truth, the right time will be different for each one of us. There is no such thing as the right time to lose your virginity. You can wait till after marriage or you can do it before. It's all up to you.

What Should I Do?

A short story

Priyanka asked me to meet her downstairs for a quick cup of chai. Unable to keep the huge grin off her face, she told me she had some news. Good news, she added. I shifted the burning hot glass of tea from hand to hand until it cooled down, and Priyanka began to tell me about her weekend.

'He called me randomly and said a few friends were going to Turquoise Cottage,' she giggled. 'We got so drunk, I mean everyone must have done like four shooters each and cocktails on top of that.'

'Wow,' I exclaimed, adding, 'I hate shooters.'

'Yeah, me too, actually. But everyone kept insisting. Anyway, then we dropped his friends off…'

'You drove,' I interrupted, 'while you were that drunk?'

'He drove and it wasn't far. Anyway, then we went to his parents' office and stuff kind of happened there.'

'Oh yeah? Like what?'

'Umm. This and that.'

'Did you go all the way, Priyanka?'

'No, no. But we did everything but…'

'What does that mean?'

'You know, like *everything*. It was the first time I was entirely naked with a guy.'

'Then what happened?'

'Well, we got up at about six the next morning and he dropped me back.'

'Wow, dude. So what does this mean? Are you guys together now?'

'Umm, no. He said he was still in love with his ex. So we'll just keep on seeing each other, umm, casually.'

'Really? He said he was still in love with his ex? He said that to you? That's pretty insensitive, isn't it?'

'Well, we're just friends. And I am not sure I am ready for a relationship either. But when do you think the right time to do *it* is? I mean, is he the right person? Should I do it with him?'

Who Is the Right Person?

What do you think Priyanka should do? It's hard to say if there is such a thing as the 'right person' to lose your virginity to. You have to make that decision for yourself. But here are a few things you could ask yourself to get a little closer to the answer.

- Is he willing to use a latex condom? Once you establish this, make a decision. It's hard to believe, but even in the 21st century when most people know about HIV and pregnancies, they still won't use a condom.
- Are you sober? Having one drink is fine to lose the nerves but we make our best decisions when we are sober and sans alcohol.
- Are you comfortable? Did you consent fully to everything that is happening? Is he forcing you at any point? Are you 100 per cent sure? If not, you can say NO at any time and do not have to have sex if you do not feel happy or comfortable with it at any point. Just say NO.

- Do you trust the person you want to sleep with? Unfortunately, some boys will tell their friends about it. Are you sure he will keep your secret?
- Find somewhere private. The last thing you want is for your friends to find you, or worse – your dad! So do yourself a favour and make sure you are alone, safe and secure.

Consent

Consent is when you are in complete agreement with what's happening. You have said it's okay for someone to touch you, kiss you or even have sex with you. You can stop them whenever you like or whenever you feel uncomfortable. This is your legal right. If someone does not have your consent, then they are in danger of breaking the law. The legal age of consent in India is 16 years, which means anybody below this age cannot legally say yes to sex. But even after this age, if someone touches you without your permission, without your consent, then they are breaking the law.

If someone has sex with you without your consent, this is considered rape. If someone touches or kisses you without your consent, you are being sexually assaulted. That means they are doing something illegal and you do not have to tolerate this. If something like this ever happens to you, you must tell someone you trust – maybe your mother, a sister or a friend. See the resources chapter for more information on who else you can talk to.

To Have Sex or Not to Have Sex?

Boys and Sex

'Why do men only want to get physical with a girl?' Smiti

Guys can seem like a different species when it comes to things like sex. The brutal truth is that they do not have as much to lose as women when it comes to sexual activity. For example, we can get pregnant, our parents might freak out, we risk being called names like 'slut' or 'loose'. Also, boys may not associate as much emotion with sex as we do and may have different expectations from sex.

Having said that, it's not true that *all* boys just want sex. There are plenty of boys out there who value a loving relationship and will respect you no matter what. Boys are often under pressure to have sex themselves – being a virgin when you are a boy is considered 'uncool' and so they are usually in a rush to have sex. As a result, they can come up with a million different lines to get you into bed.

A Million and One Lines Guys Will Come Up With to Sleep with You

Boys are often quite eager to have sex and will sprout some pretty funny things to try and get you into bed. Beware, and try not to fall for one of these cheesy lines.

- **If you loved me, you would sleep with me.** Having sex with someone doesn't necessarily mean you have to be in love with the person. Besides, if he is going to talk about love, then surely he would be willing to respect your decision to wait... right?

- **Sex will bring us closer.** A close relationship with someone usually comes from friendship, trust and communication, not from sex. Clue him in.
- **Everyone is doing it. We're the only ones not doing it.** So what? If everyone jumped off a bridge, would you? Besides, contrary to what he thinks, not everyone is doing it. Many couples decide to wait till they are *both* ready.
- **I am going to marry you so what's the big deal?** The big deal is that you are not yet ready and if he respects and loves you then he should wait. Besides, what guarantee is there that he will marry you?
- **If you won't give it to me then I will have to go looking for it somewhere else.** This is a threat! Someone who threatens you into having sex is not someone who cares about you. Ditch him.
- **Couples need to have sex to see if they are compatible.** While physical compatibility is an important part of a relationship, it is more important to see if you are compatible on a mental level first. Good relationships are based on friendship, trust and communication as well as physical compatibility.
- **We're both virgins so there is no danger of STDs.** Well, I got news for you! Even virgins can carry STDs. Penetrative sex is not necessary to transmit certain STDs. Some STDs can be transmitted from genital contact or even through kissing. Check out Chapter 8 for more information.

- **You don't want to do it because you are uptight/ old-fashioned/conservative.** A classic line and another bullying tactic.
- **Let's just take our clothes off, rub against one another and see what happens.** And the next thing you know, he will be pressuring you to go all the way. And when you are aroused and carried away by the moment, you are much more likely to say yes. But the decision to have sex should be a measured one and not taken lightly. You need to think about it for yourself, talk it over with your partner, see if you are both ready and, most importantly, have some protection with you.

How to Say No to Sex

'After my boyfriend kisses me, he always feels sexed up and says he wants to have sex. He never forces me but I don't want to do it.' Shilpa

Remember that you are totally within your rights to say no at any time. Even if you have done lots of physical stuff with your boyfriend, you don't have to have sex. You stop when you want to and only do things you are comfortable with.

Here are some tips to help you tell him to back off:

- **Be firm.** Stick to your guns. Don't back down even for a second, even if he pulls out his puppy dog look or says he loves you. No means no.
- **Be honest.** Tell him what your reasons are. If he respects you, he will listen and try to understand.

- **Be savvy.** If he tries to pull the old 'if you loved me, you would sleep me with me' trick, answer him back with 'Well, if you loved me, you would wait till I am ready.' Ha!
- **Be confident.** You are sure of yourself and know what you want, right? Then have faith in yourself that the decision not to have sex right now is a good one for you. Don't let anyone tell you that it's not the right decision. Remember that only *you* have the right to make any decisions about your body.
- **Be ready.** If your boyfriend starts to pull you to him, saying he wants to do it, push him back physically and leave the room as soon as possible. Do not put yourself in unnecessary danger at any time.

How to Say Yes to Sex

'The idea of "sex" has often popped into my mind, but I have never had the guts to try it with my boyfriend. Do you feel I should go for it as a part of experience?' Divia

Having sex for the first time is a big decision and you should take your time deciding when the right time is for you. Lots of girls I have spoken with ask whether they should be having sex because it seems like everyone else is. It's easy to feel pressured by your friends, your boyfriend, magazines and TV, but the decision to have sex or not is yours and yours alone.

At the same time, wanting to have sex with someone you love is totally natural and nothing to feel embarrassed or guilty about. Talk it over with your partner and make the decision together.

If you do decide you are ready, take a look at the checklist below before you launch into Planet Sex. These are just guidelines –*you* are the only one who can make this decision.

1. Do you have a condom? Do you have the confidence to buy one if your boyfriend cannot? Having sex without using a condom is as dangerous as trying to cross the road with your eyes closed.
2. Is your boyfriend willing to use a condom?
3. Do you know how to use a condom correctly? (See Chapter 7 for step-by-step instructions on how to put a condom on correctly.)
4. Will he stick by you if something goes wrong and the condom breaks?
5. Do you know how to deal with it if the condom breaks? Do you know what your options are?
6. What are your expectations of the relationship? Are you clear about where you stand with this person?
7. Do you know and trust your partner? Do you know his sexual history?
8. Can you trust him to maintain your privacy and not brag to his friends about it?
9. Are you sexually attracted to him? Does he turn you on?
10. Do you care for him? You don't have to love someone to have sex with them but it will feel a lot nicer if you have some feelings for each other.
11. Do you feel like you are being forced into sex? Is your boyfriend putting pressure on you to have sex with him? Do you feel like you have to have sex because everyone else is doing it?

12. Do you have somewhere safe and private to go to do it?
13. In the worst case scenario, what would your parents do if they found out?

Sexual Activity

Sexual activity means that you are involved in some form of touching or fondling involving genitalia with another person. Masturbating does not make you sexually active.

It's a good idea to read Chapter 7 on protection before engaging in any sexual activity. Know what the risks are, what your options are and you will enjoy sex much more. The most important thing to remember if you are sexually active is the responsibilities that come with it.

When you realize that you want to be sexually active, take it step by step. Test the boundaries a little every time, seeing what you are comfortable with and what you enjoy. You may want to stop at any time and this is perfectly okay. Being sexually active can be very enjoyable, but you have to make sure you are relaxed, happy and comfortable.

First, Let's Get Some Questions Out Of the Way...

What Is an Orgasm?

An orgasm is the climax of sexual tension. It can come from having sex with someone, masturbation or even from having a sexy dream. Some women ejaculate from their urethra but this rarely seeps out of the vagina. During an orgasm, your vagina might contract or quiver a little as the muscles relax, your nipples become erect and you might feel warm all over. When a man orgasms, he also feels warm and tingly all over. It is widely accepted that men reach orgasm more easily than women, and, for men, ejaculating and reaching orgasm are two different processes. But this chapter aims to show you that it's also perfectly possible for you to reach orgasm every time you have a sexual encounter.

What Is Semen?

Semen is the fluid that is ejaculated from a man's penis when he comes/orgasms. It contains sperm which is what fertilizes a woman's egg and makes her pregnant.

How Long Can Sperm Live in a Woman's Body?

Sperm can live in a woman's body for 5-7 days after sex.

What Usually Happens to Semen After Sex? Does it Stay in the Body?

If you used protection, the semen will collect in the tip of the condom and you should be careful while removing the condom so that it doesn't drip out. If you are not using a condom, then the semen mostly drips out of your body, although a small amount is absorbed by the body too. You may notice a small discharge when you next urinate or find a small white dicharge in your panties, and this could be a small amount of the come/ semen seeping out of your body.

Remember, it's important to use a latex condom if you are having sex with someone. See Chapter 7 for more information on condoms.

Kissing

This is when you bring your lips together with another person. We might kiss our parents or friends on the cheek but kissing on the mouth is usually saved for our boyfriend or girlfriend. Most people worry whether they are a good kisser or how their first kiss will go, so here are a few pointers on how to make it an enjoyable experience.

- Relax. Come on, this is a nice thing. If you are a bundle of nerves, you will forget to enjoy it. Take a long, deep breath and go for it.
- Lean your head in, tilted slightly to one side.
- Close your eyes just before you touch his/her lips.
- Make sure your lips are a little moist – have a glass of water beforehand or lick your lips just before you kiss.
- When you make contact, part your lips a little and gently position your lower lip between his/her lips.
- Now your lips are interlocked and you can use your tongue to explore a little. But go slow and be gentle.
- Don't just rub his/her teeth with your tongue. Play a little with his/her tongue, using your tongue.
- You can either place your hands on the back of his/her head or on his/her back and move them slowly in circular motions.

Things might get a little steamier at this point. He/she might lick and kiss your neck a little or you might want to do the same to them. Your neck is one of the most sensitive areas on your body and having someone touch and kiss it can feel great.

What's Happening to My Body at this Time?

Your body is being sexually stimulated. You'll probably feel desire and your vagina might get a little wet. Your adrenalin is pumping, and your body is alert and responsive.

Breasts

'Is it okay to let your boyfriend touch your breasts while you have your clothes on?' Sheetal

Your breasts are very sensitive and it can feel very nice if someone touches them the right way. The best way to find out what you like is to do it yourself. Feel your breasts, circle your nipples with your fingertips. Does that feel nice? Squeeze your nipples. Does that hurt? Or feel nice? Once you have figured out what you like, tell your partner or show them.

It would be a lie to say that boys don't like breasts. They like them a lot so they will be keen to touch and suck them. If you feel comfortable and like the way it feels, this is no big deal. You cannot get pregnant, contract HIV or even lose your virginity by someone touching your breasts.

Rubbing Against One Another with Your Clothes On

Stimulating your sex organs by rubbing against one another with no direct skin contact poses no risk for STDs or pregnancy. And it can also feel very nice.

Rubbing

Rubbing is when we use the palm of our hand or our partner's hand to stimulate the clitoris. This very sensitive body part is located under the mons pubis, the area directly above the vagina that is covered in pubic hair (see Chapter 2 for more information). When women masturbate, they commonly massage this area, as directly below it is the most sensitive part of your genitals – the clitoris – and it is usually the stimulation of the clitoris that leads to an orgasm. You can ask your partner to use his/her hand to massage you in circular motions in this area until you orgasm.

Research has shown that most women only orgasm by being rubbed and not through penetrative sex. This is because the clitoris is located in a place that is hard to reach with the penis. Having an orgasm from someone rubbing your mons pubis is nothing to feel embarrassed or worried about. In fact, rubbing is one of the most satisfying and safe ways to explore your sexuality.

Fingering

Fingering is when someone puts their fingers inside your vagina and moves them in and out. Or he/she might run their fingers along the outside of your vagina. You will probably get wet if you are aroused. If you find your vagina is still dry, it could be because you are nervous or not comfortable. Also, vaginal lubrication can come and go – it isn't necessarily an indication of the level of your arousal.

Risks

Here are a few simple rules that should be followed to make sure fingering remains safe and fun for both of you:

- Make sure his/her hands have been washed with soap.
- Make sure his/her nails are cut very short and are clean. Dirty fingernails can cause infection and long nails can cut you.
- If he/she has a cut on their finger, make sure they put a plaster on first.
- He/she should wash their hands before putting them in your mouth again.

It is possible to put your fingers in someone's anus as well. But if you decide to do this, you must make sure you wash your hands or make sure your partner washed their hands thoroughly before putting them in your vagina or your mouth. There is a large risk of bacteria transferring from one orifice to the other and this can cause infections like thrush (see Chapter 8).

Hand Job

You can also bring a man to orgasm by giving him a hand job. This means you use your hands to masturbate him.

Things to Remember

Just like the vagina, the penis is sensitive and should always be treated gently and with care. Make sure your hands are clean. Remove any rings as this might catch on his skin and hurt him.

Risks

There is little risk involved in a hand job. You cannot get pregnant. But if you have a small cut on your hand and he has a cut on his penis or he comes on your hand and either of you have an STD, like HIV or hepatitis, there is a risk that the disease may be transmitted.

Mutual Masturbation

This is when you give him a hand job and he rubs or fingers you at the same time. You can both come to orgasm without actually having penetrative sex. Mutual masturbation is very popular with most couples because of the low risks involved. Avoid any contact with your vagina while you have semen on your hands or make him wear a condom.

Oral Sex

Oral sex is widely practised around the world because it is believed that it is a safer way to be sexually active. This is partly true and partly false. There is no risk of pregnancy with oral sex but there is still a risk of contracting sexually transmitted diseases like HIV, so you have to be careful and choose someone you trust to do it with.

It is possible to catch chlamydia, human papillomavirus (HPV), gonorrhea, herpes, hepatitis (multiple strains), and other sexually transmitted diseases – including HIV – through oral sex. See Chapter 8 for more information on STDs.

Penetrative Sex

What is penetrative sex?

Penetrative sex is when a penis enters a vagina.

What exactly happens when you have sex?

When a woman and a man have penetrative sex, he puts his erect penis into her vaginal hole. There are several positions in which to have sex but the most common is the missionary position, which is where the woman is on the bottom with her legs spread wide apart and the man lies on top so that his legs are in between hers.

Both the woman and man should be turned on to have sex, which can be achieved through foreplay – by kissing, touching breasts, fingering and even oral sex. The vagina needs to be wet so that the penis can pass through easily and the penis needs to be erect and hard so that it can enter the vagina.

You may have to use your hand to guide the penis into the vagina. Sometimes it might take a few gentle thrusts before the penis can enter the vagina completely. Then the man moves his hips so that his penis moves up and down inside the vagina without ever fully withdrawing. They may move in this way until one or both reach orgasm.

Risks

There are significant risks in engaging in penetrative sex. One of the easiest ways to contract an STD, especially HIV, is through bodily fluids like semen. So you should always wear a condom.

Also, pregnancy is a huge risk. Again, wearing a condom can reduce the risk of pregnancy by almost 95 per cent if you use it properly. See Chapter 7 for more information on how to put a condom on properly, and other ways you can protect yourself from pregnancy and STDs.

Your Questions on Sex Answered

'Is it necessary for a woman to orgasm to get pregnant?' Kanta

Not at all – you can get pregnant at any time while you are ovulating if you are engaging in unprotected sexual intercourse.

'Does a woman orgasm every time she has sex?' Manju

It depends. Many women do not orgasm from penetrative sex but by massaging their vulva from the outside. Rubbing the clitoris (see Chapter 2 for more information on the vulva) and the mons pubis can bring a lot of women to orgasm more easily than having a penis inside the vagina.

Through masturbation, women can figure out what they like and what brings them to orgasm and then let their partner know this. A good idea is to guide your partner's hand and show him what you like. Put his hand on top of yours and show him where to put it. Do not be embarrassed. He probably wants to please you and will be glad you showed him how you like it.

'I am a virgin and worry about having sex for the first time. I'm worried I won't be good at it.' Beatrice

'Performance' is something everyone worries about – both men and women – no matter how experienced they are. A 40-year-old woman who is married with kids might still worry about her performance. And remember that everyone has a first time. We are all 'new' to sex at some point in our lives and while your partner may pretend he/she knows more than you do, he/she is probably just as worried about not knowing what to do. Fumbling around and figuring out what to do can be part of the fun. If anything embarrassing happens, laugh it off. Being relaxed, having fun and being mature about your decision to have sex will help to make it an enjoyable experience for both of you.

'How do you protect yourself during oral sex with a woman?' Madhu

Oral sex on a woman, or 'going down', as it's often called, involves using your mouth and tongue to penetrate or lick someone's vulva.

Going down on a woman can be fun but should be taken seriously as there are risks involved in this as well. Make sure the person who is going down on you doesn't have any cuts, sores or bleeding gums.

Use a dental dam, which acts just like a condom. This is a thin piece of latex that acts as a layer of protection between your tongue and someone's vulva. See Chapter 7 for tips on how to make your own dental dam using a condom.

'Do you need to use a condom when you have oral sex?' Bansri

There are significant risks involved in performing oral sex on a man or a woman. If you have cuts, sores or bleeding gums, these can all transmit disease and get your partner sick. So, it's better to use a condom if you are having oral sex with a man and a dental dam if you are having oral sex with a woman

'During oral sex, is it okay to swallow come?' Mital

If you have a condom on during oral sex then the come/semen will accumulate in the tip of the condom. Take the condom off carefully and tie the open end to make sure no come drips out. Now, you can throw it in the garbage.

If you do not have a condom on, it is advisable to spit out the semen. This is because if you do swallow, you could be at risk of contracting an STD if he is infected.

'Does it really hurt a lot when a girl has sex the first time?' Nikku

If the vagina is not wet enough, it might be difficult for a penis to penetrate the vagina. Take some time to touch and kiss and explore one another's bodies, and make sure you are turned on. As you grow aroused, you secrete a small amount of fluid which lubricates the vagina and makes you wet. This helps to prevent any pain when the penis enters the vagina. You should also try to be as relaxed as possible. Your vaginal opening is elastic and will stretch to accommodate a penis but it may hurt a little initially, even if you are turned on. This usually goes away with time and a little practice!

Using a condom with lubricant can also help. But never use a lubricant like baby oil or Vaseline as this can reduce the effectiveness of the condom. Always use a water-based lubricant and check the label to make sure or run it under some water – if it washes away easily, it's a water-based lubricant.

'How does the guy locate the girl's "hole"? What if he aims at the urinary hole instead? Wouldn't it hurt?' Jaya

The hole through which urine comes out is called the urethra. This is a tiny opening and there is *no* possibility of anybody putting a penis or a finger in it by mistake. The 'hole' in which a man might put his penis is lower. This opening becomes elastic during sexual activity and will stretch to accommodate a penis or someone's fingers.

'How should I behave during my first intercourse?' Urvashi

There is no right or wrong way to behave during intercourse. Most people feel a little nervous or anxious but it's also very important to relax and have fun. Talk to your partner – tell him what you like and what you don't. It's natural to feel tenderness and warmth towards the person you are having sex with. Kiss them or play with their hair to let them know you feel close to them. You can close your eyes for a while and really relax. You can laugh, talk or stay silent. Whatever you want.

'Is it necessary to have sex once you are married?' Lucky

Having sex once you are married is important, as people usually need physical as well as emotional intimacy from a relationship. If you feel attracted to your partner, you will probably want to have sex with them. With time and by communicating with your husband, you can figure out what you both like in bed and end up having a lot of fun. Some couples decide that a lot of sex is important for them and some decide it's not that important. Talking to your partner will help you decide what's right for both of you.

But you don't have to do anything you don't feel comfortable with. Being pressured or forced into sex is illegal and you should not have to put up with anything that makes you feel miserable. There is a misconception among men that they have the 'right' to have sex with their wives anytime they want. This is, of course, not true. Marital rape is a punishable crime. If you feel like you are in danger, see Chapters 9 and 10 for information on how to get help.

'Is it weird that I don't have any hang-ups about sex? I want to sleep with two different guys – is there anything wrong with me?' Pinky

Not at all. Wanting to sleep with two guys is your choice and only you can decide what's right for you. Make sure you use a condom each time and be honest with yourself and your partners. Finally, be sure that you are not using sex as a way to make guys like you. It's advisable to have sex when you are comfortable and ready, and because you care about and want to be with someone physically. Not because you think having sex is 'cool' or because you think it's the only way to get guys to notice you.

'My partner really wants to please me, but he gets offended if I don't orgasm each time so I pretend that I have. What should I do? Is it necessary for me to orgasm every time I have sex?' Monica

Faking an orgasm in order not to offend your partner is something every woman can relate to. Most women need a lot more sexual build-up than men and research indicates that it's hard to orgasm through penetrative sex alone. Many women need clitoral stimulation as well.

But faking an orgasm each time you have sex will mislead your partner into thinking you are enjoying what's happening. Unless you tell him that you are not sexually satisfied, he will continue to bang away with no consideration for you. And you can't blame him – he doesn't even know he is doing anything wrong.

For sex to be an enjoyable experience for both you and your partner, your pleasure should be a priority. But orgasms don't have to be the goal of every sexual encounter. It's all about communicating to your partner what you like and what feels good. Keep in mind that most men will find it hard to hear the truth, so be as sensitive as possible. Reassure him about how attracted you are to him, how sexy you think he is.

Also, it's a myth that couples should orgasm at the same time – this is rare and, frankly, overrated. Try using oral sex so that you can orgasm first and then continue to penetrative sex for his orgasm.

'Does a man's orgasm die earlier than a woman's or are they just satisfied more easily?' Myna

Generally speaking, men can orgasm more easily than women. This is because the penis is a visible sex organ and can be easily aroused. But the principal sex organ for a woman, the clitoris, is buried under a protective hood (the clitoral hood) and therefore harder to reach. Many women place more emphasis on foreplay and take longer to get aroused than a man. Finally, there is a lot of emphasis on the man's orgasm because of the misogynistic nature of society and because his sperm is essential for procreation.

'Is it possible to have sex during your period?' Maya

Yes. Penetrative sex during your period is possible. But unprotected sex or oral sex isn't recommended, because menstrual blood can transmit HIV and other STDs.

'Does the transmission of sperm start at the moment of insertion/intercourse or does it take time?' Khushi

A man can emit something called pre-ejaculation at any time during foreplay or sex. This fluid contains enough sperm to make a woman pregnant. But the bulk of his sperm is delivered in the form of semen. After ejaculation, his penis becomes limp, or flaccid, again.

'How can you tell if a guy loves you while having sex?' Manika

There is no easy answer to this. It really depends from person to person. There are a few things you can watch out for – for example, does he enjoy pleasuring you? Is your enjoyment his priority? Is there a lot of kissing and tenderness in the sex? Is he attentive and considerate?

But these are just general observations and not rules to be followed to figure out whether a guy loves you or not. Most importantly, ask yourself whether you are sleeping with him because you want him to love you. Choosing to sleep with someone to try and make them love you is a sure-fire way to erode your self-esteem and self-respect. Find someone more deserving of you or just ask this guy whether he is invested in the relationship or not.

I Had Sex... and Now I Have Some Questions

Regrets

'I had sex once but nobody knows about it. After that my boyfriend kind of started avoiding me. Did he get into a relationship with me only because he wanted to use me?' Shakti

We can all feel a little panicked after having sex for the first time. Some of us wonder whether we did it right, whether he enjoyed it, or whether we were safe. Just remember, it's natural to feel a little freaked out.

If your boyfriend continues to avoid you after sex, ask him what's wrong. You might find he's just embarrassed and wondering whether *he* did it right. If he still avoids you and will not talk to you, forget about him. Some boys, unfortunately, are just interested in sex and do not have the maturity it takes to handle a loving, healthy relationship. In this case, he does not deserve you. Try talking to a friend about it or maybe call one of the helpline numbers in the resources chapter at the end of this book.

Most importantly, take a deep breath and remind yourself that this is no big deal. Okay, so you had sex with someone and didn't like it much. Now you wish you hadn't done it. But it's not the end of the world, no matter how much it might feel that way. You will forget this unfortunate experience in due time.

Will My Vagina be Loose After Sex?

Not at all! Your vagina stretches to accommodate a penis. But afterwards, it returns to its normal size.

My Boyfriend Reaches Orgasm Before We Even Start to Have Sex or Almost Immediately After We Start.

This is called premature ejaculation and is very common, especially among younger boys who get really excited about the prospect of having sex and can reach orgasm very soon into the act. This might leave you feeling like you have done something wrong or that you don't have a good sex life. But as your boyfriend gets more used to the idea of having sex and becomes more in tune with his body, this should happen less often. If you find he continues to ejaculate prematurely, suggest a visit to the doctor.

He Lost His Erection in the Middle of Sex – What Did I Do Wrong?

You did nothing wrong. Boys and men can sometimes experience a loss of erection for several reasons – they are stressed, ill, tense, nervous, tired, or had too much alcohol to drink. It is no indication that he has lost interest in you or finds something wrong with your love making. It's a common problem that nearly all men experience at some point in their lives.

Be sensitive and patient. Men place a lot of emphasis on their penis and sexuality, and having a problem with erections can be a cause of great concern for them. He may feel embarrassed or nervous in front of you. Ask him if he wants to talk about it or if something is stressing him out. Be sensitive and as sympathetic as possible.

If it keeps happening and he is not able to sustain an erection, then consider visiting a doctor.

We Touched Each Other and Had Lots of Foreplay But He Never Got a Hard On. What Happened?

Again, this is no indication that he has lost interest in you. Not being able to get an erection is common and experienced by men of all ages and backgrounds. It could be a sign that he is working too hard, is stressed out, drinking too much alcohol or fallen ill. Certain kinds of medication can also affect erections.

Try resting for a while before you try again. Sometimes all he might need is a chance to calm down and relax. Reassure him that you are still attracted to him. If he is not able to get an erection over a long period of time, suggest he go see a doctor.

After We Did It, I Felt Closer and More Comfortable With Him. But He Doesn't Seem as Affectionate.

Some say that men and women tend to react differently to sex. Men typically want to sleep or leave as they might associate less emotion with sex than we do. Women might want to hug, kiss and spend the night holding one another. It is common to feel warm, loving and affectionate after sex and want to share these feelings with your lover. But if your partner does want to sleep or leave, this is no indication of how much he loves or wants you.

Everyone reacts differently to sex. Some of us feel embarrassed or shy for a variety of reasons – maybe we don't know the person that well or are worried that we did something wrong. Some of us feel sleepy, relaxed and calm. Some feel invigorated and energized. Some couples cuddle and kiss in bed after having sex while some couples roll over and go to sleep. Only you know what works for you.

Can Anyone Tell by Looking at Me That I Had Sex Last Night?

You might feel a bit sore around your vagina, but this discomfort passes in a day or so. You don't look, smell or act different once you have had sex and no one can tell by looking at you what you were up to last night.

Now That I Have Had Sex Once, Do I Have to Do It Again?

Nope. You don't have to do it again until you feel ready. Explain to your partner that you want to take a little break and sort out your thoughts. Do not feel pressured to do it every time you meet. If you prefer foreplay or just hanging out, communicate this to your partner. Tell him/her that you want to wait till you are really up for it again, if at all.

I Didn't Like It as Much as I Thought I Would.

Most of us will have a disappointing first sexual experience. It can be clumsy because no one is quite sure what to do. Some people don't realize how messy it can get! And some people realize they prefer foreplay and/or oral sex to penetrative sex. Whatever the reason, don't let it get you down. The sex will probably improve as both of you get more comfortable with the idea and with each other. But if you don't want to do it again, that's okay too.

How Do I Know if I Did It Right?

Contrary to what magazines and movies tell you, there is no 'right' way to have sex. Everyone has to find the right way for them. If you both had fun, were sexually fulfilled and comfortable, then you had a great sexual experience. Talk to your partner and ask them how they feel. Did they have fun? Do they want to try something different next time? Good communication with your partner will help you both have more fun in bed.

Could I be Pregnant?

There are several ways to tell if you might be pregnant:

- Did you use protection? If not, there is a chance you might be pregnant.
- Did the protection method fail? Did the condom break or did you miss your pill? If so, there is a chance you might be pregnant.

Remember that you can take the Emergency Contraception pill if you act quickly. Taken up to 72 hours after any sexual activity, the EC pill can prevent a pregnancy. See Chapter 7 for more information.

If you answered yes to either of the questions and more than 72 hours have passed since you had sex, you might be pregnant. Have you missed a period? If so, get yourself a pregnancy test as soon as possible. These are relatively inexpensive and available at all chemists. There is no taboo around buying pregnancy tests so don't feel embarrassed and do not wait too long. Ignoring this problem is not going to make it go away. Read the instructions on the pregnancy test carefully – you have to wait a certain amount of time after having sex before you can test yourself and shouldn't dilute your urine too much beforehand. In other words, don't drink tons of water before you take the test.

I'm Pregnant! What Do I Do Now?

If the test comes up positive, be sure to take another test in a few days just to be sure. If this second test confirms that you are pregnant, don't panic. You still have an option left – you can choose to get an abortion.

Abortion

What Is Abortion?

Abortion is a method used to empty the uterus of any foetal tissue. It effectively terminates a pregnancy. There is a lot of debate around abortion – some people believe that a child's life starts 20 weeks into a pregnancy, some disagree. But one fact that everyone agrees on is that abortion should be a last resort and only opted for when everything else has failed. Prevention is the best cure – so read Chapter 7 again and again until you are sure what contraceptive method is best for you. Having said this, unavoidable mistakes do happen and if you do find yourself with an unwanted pregnancy, read on to find out what your options are.

Why do People Have Abortions?

Seventy-eight per cent of pregnancies in India are unplanned and 11 million abortions are carried out every year. The reasons for not wanting a baby are plentiful and every woman needs to make the decision for herself. Here are some examples of why someone might want an abortion:

- Having a baby on your own is really tough. Single mothers do not usually receive much support from society.
- You cannot afford to have a baby right now – you want to study some more and you are not sure when you might get a job. Babies are very expensive!
- Having a baby will put your health in jeopardy.
- You were not prepared for the sexual encounter. If you were raped or don't trust your partner for any reason, you may not want to have a baby under those circumstances.
- Ther is something developmentally or physically wrong with the baby.

What Happens during an Abortion?

Depending on how far along you are in your pregnancy, you can visit a licensed doctor and ask for an abortion. Up to two months after your last period, you can get a medical abortion – this involves taking two sets of pills. The first set of pills will prevent your uterus from building up a lining which in turn will prevent the egg from attaching to the walls and developing into a pregnancy. After about 2-3 days, you take the second set of pills. These will cause the uterus to empty. This might be followed by some heavy bleeding and cramps.

It's worth noting that these pills are not always reliable and you should take another pregnancy test a few weeks later just to be sure. If you wait six weeks after the sexual encounter, some surgery is involved in terminating your pregnancy. So act quickly.

Leela's Abortion

A true story

Leela is five foot two and has streaked black hair. Every time she smiles, her eyes shine and two distinct dimples appear on her plump cheeks. But today she isn't smiling. She has a lot on her mind and wants to talk about it. 'My boyfriend got me pregnant last year,' she tells me.

Leela explains that they didn't use protection, he had assured her that he wouldn't ejaculate until he had withdrawn. She believed him and only when she missed her period two months in a row did she realize the consequences of the mistake.

> The withdrawal method has never proved successful. Even before a man orgasms and ejaculates fully, he emits something called pre-ejaculation, which is a tiny bit of come. This liquid contains sperm and can put you at risk for pregnancy. In addition, a man might ejaculate quicker than he expected or even lie and say that he hasn't ejaculated.

Leela and Vikas met at the Hyatt Hotel, where Vikas worked as an assistant chef and she was completing a hospitality internship. They got together a few times a week and within a month, they had sex. It was their first time together and Leela's first time ever, and she became pregnant.

> Some girls have asked me whether you can get pregnant the first time you have sex. The answer is YES! You are at risk of pregnancy *every time* you have sex, whether it's the first, tenth or last time, unless you use a condom or another contraceptive.

When Leela told Vikas that she was pregnant, he insisted on an abortion. Leela was very upset by his words. 'I was hurt but I also knew we had no other choice. My parents would kill me if they knew I was pregnant,' Leela laments.

> Does Leela have a choice? She could marry Vikas but does she really want to be in a relationship with this man for the rest of her life because of one mistake? She could have the baby and raise it herself. Or she could give the baby up for adoption. What do you think she should do? What would *you* do?

The next day she visited the gynaecology clinic she had seen in the market near her college. The doctor gave her a test and confirmed that she was pregnant. She asked if Leela was married. 'I lied and said yes,' Leela recalls. 'Because I knew that if she found out the truth, that I was a single woman and pregnant, she would not help me.' Leela told the doctor that she and her husband could not afford a child at the moment. She asked the doctor for an abortion.

Legally, the doctor would have had to give Leela an abortion even if she was single. Abortions up to 5 months/20 weeks have been legal in India since 1971. In fact, government hospitals are licensed to offer abortions for free. However, hospitals do not often follow the law. Instead, women, especially unmarried women, are treated unfairly and harassed for cash. Like Leela, most middle-class women go to private clinics for help. Unfortunately, not every gynaecologist is licensed to perform an abortion. Every year, 20,000 women die from unsafe abortions. So, you have to be careful whom you ask for help. Ask to see their licence. If you are above the age of 18, you do not need your parents' permission to get an abortion. The average cost for an abortion in Delhi is Rs 4000.

'She told me that I should keep the child, that if I had an abortion now, I might not be able to conceive again,' Leela says. But after insisting that she did not want the baby, the doctor reluctantly told Leela that she should come back the next morning. She gave her the details about the procedure – she could choose to have an abortion under general anaesthesia, which would mean no pain but would cost much more than the local anaesthesia abortion, during which she would be awake but unable to feel her bottom half. Vikas had agreed to pay so Leela decided on the general anaesthesia option.

It is a myth that if you have an abortion, you might not be able to conceive again. Legal, safe abortions do not damage your reproductive organs. However, you must make sure you have a legal abortion because doctors who do not know what they are doing can hurt and damage you in some way.

'The next morning I went to the clinic with a friend,' Leela remembers. 'She signed something saying that if anything happened to me in surgery, she would be responsible for me.'

If you are three months or less into your pregnancy, then you will probably receive what's referred to as a Medical Termination of Pregnancy (MTP). This involves taking a combination of pills, most commonly called methotrexate or mifepristone, followed by a prostaglandin (either misoprostol, gemeprost, or misoprostol). About 90 per cent of women benefit from this method. The other 10 per cent may need some surgical intervention to successfully abort the foetus.

The most common method of surgical abortion is called suction-aspiration or manual vacuum abortion (MVA). During a MVA abortion, the foetus is removed by suction using a manual syringe or an electric pump. After 15 weeks, a method called dilation and evacuation (D&E) is used. This involves opening and cleaning the cervix using surgical instruments.

She continues. 'It was a horrible experience, sitting there in the clinic, waiting to go inside. There were these two men who worked at the clinic, and I felt them looking at me, laughing, whispering,' she recounts. 'The next thing I knew, they had given me the medicine and I was asleep.'

About three hours later, Leela was discharged from the clinic, she was given a pamphlet and told to come back if she was in any pain. 'I cried and cried when I got home,' she rues. She broke up with Vikas soon after. 'He didn't even call to see if I was okay,' Leela says angrily. 'So I told him it was over.'

The physical repercussions of having an abortion can be multifaceted. Your hormones fluctuate to a great extent after an abortion – your body has been preparing for a baby and all of a sudden it has to return to the way it was before the pregnancy. This can play havoc with your emotions and make you feel a hundred different things in just one day. Emotional support after an abortion is essential but most clinics do not offer any service like this. If you have a college counsellor, talk to her. Otherwise, confide in a friend or your boyfriend about how you are feeling. There are also a few websites that you can check out for advice on how to feel better and deal with the aftermath. See Chapter 10 for more information.

A few months went by but Leela could not forget what had happened and slipped into depression. One day, her parents told her they were looking for a boy for her and wanted to get her married. She panicked, worried that her new husband would be able to tell that she had had an abortion. And that was when Leela came to see me.

'Will someone find out?' she asks, her face crumpled in anxiety. I reassure her that nobody can tell if you have had an abortion, even if they look at your vagina through a magnifying lens. She finally relaxes a little. 'But what if my husband thinks my vagina is loose?' she inquires. But Leela has nothing to worry about. The vaginal wall is a muscle and stretches all the time, so no one can tell if you have had sex a few times.

For abortions under five months, where the foetal tissue is vacuumed through the vagina, no scars are visible and no one will be able to tell whether you have had an abortion or not. Your medical records are kept completely confidential by law so the doctors will not be able to tell anyone. To be on the safe side, don't go to your family doctor; find a doctor who is not in your neighbourhood.

Leela leaves our meeting looking a little calmer. Over the next few weeks, she continues to email me, still traumatized by what she went through. I see her again six months later, almost one year after her abortion. I ask her whether she would use protection the next time she has sex. She laughs and says, 'I wish I had used it the first time. I would have avoided all of this.'

It's always, always a good idea to use a condom. And if something does go wrong, make sure you take the morning after pill/ emergency contraception pill the next day – don't ignore the issue for two months like Leela did.

Seven
PROTECTION

This chapter tells you how to keep as safe as possible during any sexual activity. We talk about all the possible contraceptive methods available, including details on how to put on a condom, where to find the contraceptive pill, what a spermicide is and how to use a female condom.

Most of us are embarrassed about going to a chemist and asking for condoms or the morning-after-pill, and that's normal. There's a lot of taboo around buying contraceptives, especially if you are a woman. People might refuse to serve you or make you feel like you are doing something wrong by asking for a condom. But if you are going to be sexually active, you *have* to learn to work around this. In the next few pages, you will find a few temporary solutions on how to get around the fear of buying contraception – you could ask a friend to go with you to the chemist, order the condoms online or ask a guy friend to get them for you. None of these is a great solution, but it might help a little. Hopefully with time, as more and more of us start asking for the things we deserve – like the right to be safe and healthy – and stand up to judgemental chemists and doctors, things like buying condoms or deciding to go on the pill will become easier.

Using a condom during all sexual activity is the most advisable form of protection. Condoms are the only form of protection that reduce the risk of contracting an STD. But pick one other method of protection to be extra safe – to make sure you are not only well-protected from STDs, but also from the risk of pregnancy. Read on to find out which of these options will suit you the best.*

Condoms

As Chapter 6 tells you, the importance of using a latex condom during every type of sexual activity cannot be underestimated. Condoms are extremely effective at protecting you from STDs and unwanted pregnancies. The most effective type of condom is a latex condom. This simple, readily available, inexpensive item made from latex rubber could even save your life.

* We have included the names of some brands available in major cities to give you an idea of what you can ask for at a chemist. It's up to you to decide which brand to use. All prices are subject to change.

Brands and Costs

There are many different types of condoms – flavoured, ribbed, dotted, and even glow-in-the-dark ones. It really depends on what you want. For example, flavoured condoms might be nice for oral sex and the glow-in-the-dark ones might add an element of fun. Ribbed and dotted condoms add a little more friction during sex but don't really make a huge difference to how a man's penis feels. Some condoms even come pre-lubricated. The most important thing is to make sure the condom is made of latex. Some novelty condoms like the glow-in-the-dark ones are made of other materials that aren't as effective as latex when it comes to preventing STDs.

The three biggest condom bands available in India are Kamasutra, Moods and Durex. Condoms are relatively inexpensive (about Rs 50 for a pack of 10 at the time this was written). Only use a condom brand that you trust and recognize.

Where to Get Them

The last thing you want is to have planned a beautiful, romantic evening together when you are finally going to do it and find that he has forgotten the condom or is too drunk to put it on properly. So, it is as much your responsibility to have a condom with you if you are planning to have sex, as it is the man's. Read on to find out where to get your condoms and make sure you carry one or two in your purse to be sexually safe at a moment's notice.

From a chemist

Buying a condom is not the easiest thing in the world. It's intimidating to go into a chemist's and ask for some. But remember that these people do not know you and will never be able to tell your parents or relatives. Pick a chemist in an area where you do not live. Go at a relatively busy time if you are worried about the owners. Ask for the brand – don't say 'Give me some condoms please.' Asking by the brand name will save you some embarrassment. And if you just can't face going in alone, ask a friend to go with you.

Besides, most chemists just want business and are happy to sell you *anything* without batting an eyelid.

Vending machines

There are several vending machines for condoms now available in major cities like Delhi, Mumbai and Calcutta, but these are relatively hard to locate.

On the net

You can order condoms online at www.moodsplanet.com or www.kamasutraontheweb.com. Shipping is free but you do have to order at least Rs 150 worth of condoms. At the moment, they only accept Mastercard and Visa credit cards. I cannot guarantee how the packages will arrive and whether people will be able to tell what the contents of the package are, although both websites promise to be discreet.

From your sex partner

If you just can't face any of this, get your partner to buy some condoms for you. It is, unfortunately, easier for boys to ask for things like condoms, and they can get away without people asking too many questions. Once he has bought some, keep one in your bag for emergencies.

How To Put a Condom on Properly

A latex condom that's used correctly will offer greater protection than one that is not used correctly. So it's worth learning how to put one on properly. And just to make sure you get it right, here is a step-by-step guide on how to put a condom on:

1. Make sure the date on the condom packet has not expired.
2. Make sure the packet isn't broken, torn, or weathered by sun damage.
3. Open the packet carefully. Do not use scissors to do this and be sure not to tear the condom.
4. Remove the condom from the packet.
5. Your partner's penis has to be erect to be able to wear a condom. If the penis is flaccid then you cannot put on a condom.
6. Place the bit that sticks out a little like a nipple at the top of the penis and pinch it lightly with your fingers (not with your nails!). This is called the tip of the condom and is used to catch the semen. You need to hold it like this to remove the air from inside the condom (so that it doesn't tear during sex).

7. Very carefully, still holding onto the tip, unroll the condom over the penis till you reach the bottom.
8. Leave some space at the top of the condom – holding the tip while you roll it down will help with this. If a condom is on too tight, it might tear during sex.
9. Make sure you do not use your nails to do any of this as it will tear the condom.
10. After sexual intercourse, the semen will be trapped in the tip of the condom so you have to be careful while taking it off.
11. Hold the tip at the bottom with your thumb and forefinger (so that all the semen is pushed to the top of the tip) and unroll the condom gently.
12. Check the condom for any tears or breaks. If you see something, you may want to consider taking the emergency contraception pill in the next 72 hours.
13. Tie a knot in the bottom of the condom and put it in a piece of tissue.
14. Throw it in the bin. Do not flush the condom as it may clog the toilet.
15. Wash your hands thoroughly.

Important Things To Remember When Using a Condom

It is best to practise a few times before doing it for real – use a banana or a candle. Don't feel embarrassed – no one has to know. Find a private moment and practise. It is an important thing to get right.

If you put the condom on the wrong way, inside-out for example, which is a very common mistake, you should throw that condom away and start with a new one. Using a new condom each time you put it on a penis is very important. A little semen could have gotten onto the condom. If you do not throw it away, the semen could get into your vagina and put you at risk for STDs or pregnancy.

Use a fresh condom each time you engage in any sexual activity. For example, use one for oral sex and another one for sexual intercourse.

Sometimes you might need to use a lubricant to make things a little smoother. But you must *never* use an oil-based lubricant with a condom as this will weaken the latex rubber from which the condom is made. For example, you should never use lubricants like Vaseline, baby oil or body cream. Do not use saliva either as your saliva can contain infectious viruses that will spread to your private parts. Instead, use a water-based lubricant like K-Y jelly, which is available in large pharmacies in major cities.

Some people think using two condoms will offer them better protection. In fact, the friction caused by the two condoms rubbing against one another will probably tear them both. So just use one and put it on properly!

SPERMICIDE

What is it and what does it do?

A spermicidal is a chemical that helps to kill sperm and can be used with male and female condoms and diaphragms and caps. Even though spermicidals are available over the counter, you should always use it with another form of protection because it is not 100 per cent effective against pregnancy. Spermicidals that contain Nonoxynol-9 should be used because this is the only ingredient that helps to kill the HIV virus.

How to apply it

The spermicide should be applied inside the vagina and also on the tip of the penis. Try applying it inside the tip of the condom so that when he puts it on, the cream covers the tip of his penis.

Dental Dams

What Is It?

A dental dam is a thin square made of latex rubber that can be used to prevent the transmission of STDs during oral sex.

How Is It Used?

Hold the dental dam over the vulva or anus and perform oral sex with the dental dam between your mouth and the vulva or anus.

This allows stimulation but protects you both from STDs.

Side Effects

There are no side effects to using a dental dam.

Will It Work?

As long as it is not punctured in any way – i.e. there are no holes – a dental dam can help prevent the transmission of STDS like genital herpes and still allow you to perform oral sex. It works very similarly to a condom.

Where Do I Get It?

Dental dams can be expensive and hard to find in India. But it's very easy to make your own dental dam using a condom.

1. Open the condom packet carefully and unroll the condom onto a clean, flat surface.
2. Use scissors to cut off both ends of the condom. Leave about six inches of the condom. Be careful as you do not want to poke any holes in the condom.
3. Carefully, cut along the side of the condom so that you can open it up into a rectangle.
4. Check it for any holes. If it seems okay, you now have a dental dam that you can use during oral sex.
5. Make sure you use a fresh condom each time you want to make a dental dam. Do not re-use the dental dam.

Today Vaginal Contraceptive

What Is It?

Today is a waxy, white rectangle tablet that is doused with a spermicidal, and, if used in addition to a condom, can act as effective protection against pregnancy and STDs.

How Is It Used?

Relax, take a deep breath and insert a tablet as far up your vagina as possible. Be gentle. Make sure you do this five minutes before you intend to have sex.

The tablet will remain effective for up to an hour after you put it in (so try not to wash up straight after sex). And you should still use a condom for extra protection.

After sex, let the tablet wash out naturally. It will either come out when you next urinate – it will come out from your vaginal opening – or when you take a shower.

Side Effects

There are almost no side effects to using Today.

Will It Work?

This method has proved very effective, with a 95 per cent success rate on average.

Where Do I Get It?

Today is available at almost all chemists and costs Rs 23.30 for five tablets (at the time of writing). Each tablet can only be used once.

Female Condoms

What Is It?

The female condom works a lot like the male condom, except that it is made from polyurethane, which is stronger than latex, the material used for the male condom. The female condom protects you against STDs, HIV and pregnancy because it covers the vagina, vulva and cervix and is a good option for those allergic to latex. Most importantly, it allows a woman to control her sexual and reproductive health. We don't have to depend on the man to buy the protection or agree to wearing a condom. Unfortunately, female condoms remain relatively unavailable in India.

How Is It Used?

Female condoms come pre-lubricated, so you don't have to worry about any friction. The condom looks a little like a plastic bag with thin, plastic rings at either end. The smaller ring goes inside the vagina. This can be inserted using your fingers. Once it's in as far as it will go, put a finger inside the condom and push the inner ring further back. The larger, thinner ring hangs outside the vagina and stretches out to cover the external genitalia, stopping any cum from entering the vagina and thus protecting you. Guide the penis into the condom. Otherwise, it could be pushed aside. You do not have to use both male and female condoms.

Where Do I Get It?

Unfortunately, female condoms are not as easily available in India as male condoms. But this is slowly changing.

From a vending machine

Female condom machines have been installed in some city nightclubs.

From a chemist

Try a big chemist. There is not as much stigma around asking for a female condom because not everyone knows what it's for.

Side Effects

There are no known side effects to using a female condom but you have to wear and use the condom properly for it to be effective. Read the instructions on the packaging carefully.

Brands and Prices

At the time of writing this book, there was only one brand of female condom available in India. Marketed by Hindustan Latex Ltd, Velvet is available in most urban cities and costs Rs 100 for three condoms.

Contraceptive Pill

What Is It?

The pill can be very effective at preventing pregnancy (99 per cent effective) if taken properly but does not offer any protection against STDs, so it should always be used in addition to a condom. Each pill usually contains extra doses of oestrogen and progesterone, which are female hormones normally found in the reproductive system of a woman. The hormones help to thicken the mucus at the entrance of the cervix, helping to prevent sperm from entering the vagina. They also thin the lining of the womb, preventing an egg from being implanted there.

How Is It Used?

The pill is taken at the same time every day. Some pills come with a placebo pill (a pill that has no medicinal value), which you take for a week so that you give your body a break from the hormonal pill. Other pill brands require you stop taking the pill for exactly a week and then remember to re-start after seven days. During this break, you will usually get your 'period' although technically your periods stop while you are taking the pill. The bleeding you might experience during this seven-day break is actually your body displaying withdrawal from the hormones it's used to receiving from the pill the other 21 days.

Different pills have different hormonal dosages, and instructions about how to use them effectively, so it's a good idea to ask your doctor about different brands and find out what will work best for you.

Where Do I Get It?

You should go see your doctor if you would like to go on the pill. This doesn't mean you have to tell her about your sex life, although it's always a good idea to be as honest as possible with your doctor. Many people go on the pill because they want to regulate their period, reduce their stomach cramps or control their acne. See Chapter 8 for guidance on how to find the right doctor for you and tips on how to talk to them about your reproductive health.

Side Effects

For the first three months after starting the pill, some girls experience side effects like sore breasts, losing or gaining weight, moodiness, headaches and nausea, or bleeding between periods. But these usually clear up after a few months. If you still feel uneasy on the pill after several months, stop taking the pill or visit your doctor for further advice.

Some research has indicated that taking the pill can reduce your risk of contracting ovarian cancer. Your risk of contracting ovarian cancer is reduced by 20 per cent for every five years you have been taking the pill, and after fifteen years, the risk is halved. On the other hand, some scientists have claimed that taking the pill consistently can be harmful. You have to make the decision that's right for you.

Smoking while on the pill can increase the probability of a blood clot forming in your body, so it is not advisable to smoke while on the pill.

Brands and Prices

There are many brands of the pill available such as Novelon, Mala-D, Nirodh, Saheli, Zaroor, Choice, Apsara, Pearl. (Prices and hormonal dosages vary so check with your chemist or doctor.)

Diaphragms/Caps

What Is It?

Diaphragms, and their smaller friend, caps, are made of latex and can be inserted into your vagina and fitted over the cervix to prevent sperm from entering the vagina.

How Is It Used?

Make sure the cap is 'concave' side up – in other words, it should look like a small bowl. Apply a spermicidal to the inside of the cap. Then squeeze the diaphragm/cap together so it becomes compact and insert it into your vagina. Push until it will go no further. It should be against your cervix to be effective. It should not be removed for six hours after sex. You can then wash it, dry and store it. Each time you use it, you must reapply a generous dose of spermicidal.

Where Do I Get It?

Diaphragms and caps are available only through your doctor or gynaecologist. See the end of this chapter for information on finding a doctor who's right for you.

Side Effects

Diaphragms and caps are quite hard to put on properly, and if you do not do it right, you will be unprotected. In other parts of the world, the first time you use a diaphragm or cap, you have to visit your doctor to make sure it has been inserted correctly before you can start using it. In India, this is not the case so you should really know what you are doing. It has also been reported that some diaphragm users can contract cystitis more easily.

Brands and Prices

It's best to see your doctor about what brands are available.

IUD (Interauterine Device)

What Is It?

It is a small T-shaped device made of copper that is inserted into your vagina by a doctor. An IUD can last up to seven years although it's advisable to change your IUD every 3-4 years. The IUD acts as a barrier to pregnancy. It does not protect you against HIV or any other STD and should always be used in addition to a condom.

How Is It Used?

A doctor has to insert it. Your period is the best time to do this because your cervix is softer at this particular time and more flexible. Do not attempt to insert it yourself.

Where Do I Get It?

You can only get it from a doctor or a family planning clinic, and you need a doctor to insert it for you.

Side Effects

Most women find that their periods last longer and are heavier. You may also notice some spotting (which is when tiny spots of blood appear between your last period and your next one) or increased discharge. Some women find the insertion of the IUD painful. If you don't feel comfortable at any time, ask the doctor to remove the IUD – its effects are completely reversible and it can be removed at any time. Finally, the insertion of an IUD has been linked to an increased risk of pelvic inflammatory disease (see Chapter 8 for more information), and this risk is greatest up to three weeks after insertion.

Brands and Prices

Cu-200 is a local brand and costs Rs 250. Multiload 375 is an international brand and is easier to insert; it costs Rs 413. Again, it's best to see your doctor about the available brands and what will suit you best.

Emergency Contraception Pill (EC Pill)/Morning After Pill (MAP)

A Note: The EC pill should only be reserved for emergencies and should not be used in place of your normal contraceptive method. Frequent use can cause menstrual problems so only take it if you really have to. It does not protect against STDs and if you have had unprotected sex, you should get yourself tested for infections as well as take the set of pills. Emergency Contraception reduces the possibility of pregnancy for 72 hours (three days) after a sexual act.

What Is the EC Pill?

The EC pill can help prevent an unwanted pregnancy. Depending on where you are in your cycle, it helps prevent the egg from being fertilized or being implanted in the womb. But if the egg is already implanted, which means you are effectively pregnant, then the EC pill cannot do anything for you – it is not an abortion pill.

When Should It Be Used?

An EC pill can be taken within 72 hours of a sexual act if

- the condom breaks or tears
- you have not used protection at all
- you have been raped
- your other method of contraception failed

How Do I Take It?

Swallow one EC pill with a meal within 72 hours of the sexual act. It can cause some nausea and vomiting. If you vomit within three hours after taking the pill, then take another one with a meal or large snack.

Where Do I Get It?

You do not need a medical check-up or even a prescription to get the pill. You can buy it over the counter from any local chemist.

Will It Work?

The sooner you take the pill after the sexual act, the better it will work. If you think the condom tore, or you didn't use one, or someone raped you, take the pill as soon as possible. For the first 24 hours after unprotected sex, the pill is 95 per cent effective but the effectiveness diminishes as time goes by. For example, 24-48 hours after the sexual act it is only 85 per cent effective, and if taken 49-72 hours later, the EC pill is only 58 per cent effective.

Side Effects

Headaches, nausea, tenderness around the breasts are normal side effects but usually clear up after 24 hours. You might notice some blood in your panties or your period cycle might be a little irregular for one month but this is also normal and will clear up quickly.

Brands and Prices

EC pills cost approximately Rs 75-100. There are several brands available: I-pill, NorLevo, Cystolog, Mifegest, Pill 72, Levogestronol, Orral, Mis-take.

Abstinence

This is when a person chooses not to have penetrative sex. You choose to engage in other sexual activity but stop before having actual intercourse. Some people opt for abstinence because of their religion, which might forbid pre-marital sex, or because of their moral beliefs. The decision to wait or not to wait is entirely yours. Just remember, if you do engage in other types of sexual activity, like oral sex, you should still use a condom.

Rhythm Theory

Some people claim that there is a 'natural' way to prevent pregnancy. In other words, an egg is released 14 days after the first day of your period and so only after the egg is released can you get pregnant. There are several problems with this theory.

- The egg is never released *exactly* in the middle of the month so you can never be absolutely sure. Everything is an estimate.
- You start counting the day your period starts and not when it ends – many people get this wrong.
- You are not protected from HIV and STDs if you follow this method.

You should always, always, always use a latex condom. Even during your period or two days after your period you are still at risk of contracting HIV. The only method that truly works is using a condom.

Withdrawal Method

This is when a man and woman have sex without a condom and the man withdraws his penis just before he is going to ejaculate. Many couples believe that this prevents pregnancy. But this method has never proved effective and you are putting yourself at great risk if you choose to follow it. Firstly, not wearing a condom means you are unprotected against STDs and HIV. Secondly, when a man first gets erect, he emits a small amount of fluid called pre-ejaculation. This contains enough sperm to get you pregnant. Thirdly, even if a man says he will withdraw in time, he may not be able to! He might get carried away, or lie to you. In conclusion, the withdrawal method is not an effective method of contraception.

Eight

SEXUALLY-TRANSMITTED DISEASES

Sex can be exciting and amazing. It can make you feel on top of the world. But it can also be dangerous and needs to be taken seriously. Why? Because being sexually active can have far-reaching consequences on your life and health. It's vital to be as clued in as possible into the world of sex. For example, do you know what to do if you become pregnant? Or if you get an STD? Or contract HIV? Do you know that HIV leads to AIDS, which is deadly? All these circumstances can be avoided by reading up on the risks of STDs and how you can protect yourself.

At the time of writing this book, India has one of the highest HIV rates in the world. And young people are the ones most at risk. This is hard to believe when you realize that something as simple as using a condom could save so many lives.

You cannot tell if someone has an STD just by looking at them or their genitals. Most STDs don't even show any symptoms for several months so it's almost impossible to know if someone has something you do not want to catch. This is why it is always advisable to wear a latex condom when engaging in any sexual activity and to get tested regularly if you are sexually active.

Unfortunately, some STDs don't show up even on tests and some show no symptoms at all. Also, you do not need to have actual penetrative sex to get an STD. Sometimes all you need is skin to skin contact. The best preventive for STDs is to arm yourself with as much information as possible and to practise safe sex. See Chapter 7 for more information on the importance of sexual health.

This chapter is straightforward and easy to read. Each STD is explained in detail, with information on how you can catch it, how to spot it, and how to prevent it. Even though this book is for girls, we included the symptoms a man might experience if he has an STD – that way, you know what to watch out for. We have a not-to-be-missed section on HIV and an enlightening box on how to find a doctor and speak to him/her about your sexual life. We also give you information on common women's health issues, like thrush, and offer simple advice on how to better cope with these conditions. Read on…

Bacteria-based Diseases

Gonorrhoea

Modes of transmission

Unprotected vaginal, oral or anal sexual activity. Performing oral sex on an infected man can lead to throat-based gonorrhoea. Kissing and oral sex on women is less likely to transmit the disease but still carries some risk.

Symptoms

Women: You may not have any symptoms at all. If you do have symptoms, they may appear as more vaginal discharge than usual, a burning sensation when you urinate, or irregular periods. The symptoms take much longer to appear in women than they do in men so you may not know you have the STD until it has reached an advanced stage.
Men: Yellow, thick discharge from the penis. When urinating, it might burn. Painful, swollen testicles.

Protection

Condoms during all sexual activity. A dental dam during oral sex. See Chapter 7 to learn how to make your own dental dam with a non-lubricated condom.

What should I do if I think I have it?

Go to see your doctor as soon as possible. Ninety per cent of gonorrhoea cases are cleared up with a simple course of antibiotics. But it's important to catch it early. Undetected gonorrhoea can cause pelvic inflammatory disease (PID) in women, which may leave you sterile.

Syphilis

Syphilis is the most common STD in Delhi. It thrives in urban areas because of the close proximity in which people live. Thankfully, it's an STD that shows its symptoms early and in places that are easily visible. Be sensible and get treatment early.

Modes of transmission

Unprotected vaginal, oral or anal sexual activity. You can also get it if you touch an infectious sore.

Symptoms

A hard, round sore or ulcer will appear at the place that is infected, like your vagina or your mouth. The ulcer is painless and you may be tempted to ignore it at first, but if left untreated, syphilis advances to a second stage where a rash appears on the skin, mostly little red bumps that ooze some discharge. You might also feel like you have the flu. If you ignore this as well, the disease can reach the third stage where an ulcer might appear on one of your internal organs. You are now at risk of heart failure or a collapse of the nervous system, leading to possible death. What is particularly scary about syphilis is that after the first and second stage the symptoms might disappear altogether, so you forget about it and think that nothing is wrong. But the disease could still be within your system.

Protection

Always use a condom. If you see someone with a sore that matches the description above, do not engage in sexual activity with them (even with a condom on).

What should I do if I think I have it?

Go to see your doctor as soon as possible. Show her one of your sores. She will extract some discharge and get it checked. Syphilis is treated with penicillin, an easily available antibiotic and, if caught in time, the disease should clear up completely.

Chlamydia

Modes of transmission

Unprotected vaginal or anal sexual activity. If a bodily fluid from someone with chlamydia gets in your eye, it can lead to infection. Oral sex with an infected partner can also infect the throat.

Symptoms

Women: Women not experience any symptoms if they have chlamydia. If you do, the symptoms may appear as pain during urination; discharge; irregular periods; and the pelvis might hurt.

Men: You may not notice any symptoms. But if there are symptoms, they might include a discharge from the penis; burning or itching around the opening of the penis when urinating; anal bleeding if you had anal sex with an infected partner.

Chlamydia is sometimes called the 'silent disease' because people don't always experience symptoms and can remain untreated. Meanwhile, they might infect other people without even knowing they are spreading the disease.

Protection

Always use a latex condom while engaging in any type of sexual activity.

What should I do if I think I have it?

Women who are sexually active should be tested once a year. The test is painless and harmless.

Viruses

Genital Herpes

This is very common in urban areas in India. People live close by and interact frequently, which helps to spread the disease quickly.

Modes of transmission

Unprotected vaginal, anal or oral sexual activity. If you touch the infected area on someone's body and then touch any part of your body, you can transfer the disease, although in order for this to occur, the contact needs to happen within seconds. Someone with herpes on their lips (one of the most common areas) giving you oral sex will spread the disease to your genitals.

Symptoms

Women: Some women do not experience any symptoms. But you might notice some red bumps around the vulva, thighs or bottom. The bumps will turn into blisters that can be very painful and might burst, leaking a pus that is infectious. You might also feel some pain when urinating; have a fever; find a discharge from your vagina; experience aches and pains or swollen glands.

Men: Men may have symptoms similar to those of women or not experience any symptoms at all.

Protection

A condom should be worn at all times. However, if the sore is on your partner's fingers and he/she touches your genitals, not even a condom is going to be able to protect you.

What should I do if I think I have it?

Unlike bacterial diseases like gonorrhoea or chlamydia, one cannot treat viruses like genital herpes with antibiotics. Once you contract herpes, you have it for life.

Some anti-viral drugs can help with the discomfort but nothing can cure herpes. The first 'outbreak' or appearance of spots/blisters is usually the worst and you can have up to five outbreaks in the first year. However, over time you can expect fewer outbreaks.

Genital Warts

Modes of transmission

Unprotected sexual contact; skin to skin contact; touching an infected towel or piece of clothing (although this is very unlikely).

Symptoms

Women: You may experience no symptoms. If you do, you may notice small, painless warts that look like cauliflowers around the anus, around the vulva or inside the vagina.
Men: Men usually show no symptoms at all for genital warts but if they do, they are similar to what women experience.

Protection

Wearing a latex condom will help but genital herpes is highly infectious and the virus can exist on your partner's thighs or scrotum, so a condom will not protect you from these areas.

What should I do if I think I have it?

Contact your doctor as soon as possible. Genital warts are considered harmless. But it's advisable to get a regular pap smear – a painless, harmless test whereby a doctor gathers and tests cells from your cervix. This test will help determine if there are any genital warts on your cervix. Studies have shown that if found on the cervix, genital warts can increase your chances of contracting cervical cancer. You can freeze the warts or brush them with medicated alcohol which will cause them to fall off eventually. But this can only be done by a medical professional – do not try to remove them yourself.

Hepatitis B

Modes of transmission

Unprotected anal, vaginal or oral sexual activity; transfusion with infected blood; sharing contaminated needles; contaminated saliva, menstrual blood, nasal mucus or semen.

Symptoms

Women: You may experience no symptoms or your skin or eyes may turn yellowish (jaundiced); you might vomit or have some pain in your abdomen.
Men: Like women, men may experience no symptoms, but if they do, they will be similar to those described for women.

Protection

Using a condom during all sexual activity will help but hepatitis B is very contagious and it is advisable to abstain from sexual contact with an infected person.

What should I do if I think I have it?

Go to see your doctor as soon as possible. Again, there is no straightforward cure to this virus but your doctor will advise you to rest, drink lots of fluids and may even start you on a course of antibiotics to help with the discomfort.

HIV/AIDS

Anjali Gopalan, director of the Naz Foundation, a pioneering non-profit organization working to educate people on safe sex, tells us about HIV and AIDS.

How is HIV transmitted?

HIV stands for Human Immunodeficiency Virus. Once a person contracts HIV, the virus stays in their body for the rest of their lives. It gradually weakens the immune system so that the body eventually finds it difficult to fight off infections. When the body can no longer battle infections, the HIV virus has progressed to AIDS. There is no vaccine for HIV and there is no known cure. But infected persons can use a combination of medicine and healthy living to live long, healthy lives.

The HIV virus passes from one person to another only through body fluids. There are five bodily fluids that carry the HIV virus: pre-come, semen, vaginal fluids, breast milk and blood.

HIV can be transmitted in a number of ways:

- **Unprotected sexual contact.** Vaginal, anal or oral sex without a latex condom can infect either partner. Although the risk of infection is lower with oral sex, you are still at risk if you have a cut in your mouth or are giving oral sex to a woman who is having her period. Any exchange of bodily fluid (whether there is penetration or not) can put you at risk of HIV.
- **Blood**. If you are injected with infected blood or share

needles with someone who has the virus, you are at a high risk for contracting HIV.

- **Mother to child**. An HIV positive woman can pass the virus to her child during pregnancy, at childbirth or through breastfeeding.

HIV cannot be transmitted through casual contact such as kissing, sharing a plate, toilet seat or towel, use of public facilities (like swimming pools, theatres or bathrooms), sharing drinks or utensils. Insect bites, including mosquitoes, *do not* transmit HIV.

Symptoms

Women and Men: Some people display flu-like symptoms (sore throat, aching muscles or fever) for a short period after they contract the virus but most people see no difference in their health at all. A lot of people aren't even aware that they are infected until the virus develops into AIDS and severely affects their body's immune system. This is when you might start to lose weight, develop lesions on your body, feel tired all the time and get feverish. Eventually, the AIDS virus attacks your immune system, leaving you susceptible to other infections, like pneumonia which can then kill you.

The only way to know for sure whether you have been infected with HIV is to go for a test. If you have recently had unprotected sex, shared needles with someone, shared sex toys with someone or have another sexually transmitted infection, it is advisable you get tested for HIV as soon as possible.

How can I protect myself from HIV?

There are many things you can do to protect yourself from HIV. First, get tested so that you know your status. Second, every time you have oral, vaginal or anal sex, use a latex condom. You can also use a spermicidal (see Chapter 7) which will offer further protection. If you engage in oral sex, avoid your partner ejaculating in your mouth and do not give oral sex to a woman when she is on her period or if you have any cuts, sores or ulcers in your mouth. Do not brush your teeth or floss straight after or right before oral sex because doing so might give you small cuts in your mouth through which HIV can be transmitted. If you inject drugs, do not share needles, and use a clean needle every time.

Get tested for HIV, especially if you are pregnant or are considering getting pregnant.

Where can I go for a HIV test?

You can get an HIV test at a VCTC (Voluntary Counselling and Testing Centre). There are many VCTCs in government hospitals in all major cities in India. See the resources chapter for more information.

What happens during the test?

It's a good idea to go to a recommended, reputable clinic to get tested. Some clinics in India offer counselling along with testing and it's a good idea to ask for some time with a medical professional. They will explain the implications of the results – whether positive or negative – and offer sensitive advice about your options. Then they will ask for written consent. They cannot force you to take the test.

If you agree, a small dose of blood will be drawn from you and tested for HIV. This test should only be administered with your permission and the results given to you in confidence. By law, you are the only person who should know your test result – it is up to you whom you share it with.

In 2-3 days you can return to the VCTC to receive your results.

Are the results of my test confidential?

Both the results of your test and the fact that you got tested are kept completely confidential. At the VCTC they do not use names, only an ID number which they will issue.

How much do they charge?

The HIV test is free of charge.

Is there any treatment I can take immediately if I think I have just come into contact with HIV?

If you believe you have come into contact with HIV in a clinical setting (for example, as a health worker) it is recommended that you receive a dose of antiretroviral treatment to prevent HIV transmission.

If you have been raped or forced to have sexual intercourse against your will, see a doctor immediately. You will also receive a dose of antiretroviral treatment, as well as other medication to prevent the spread of STDs.

It is not 100 per cent guaranteed that the medication will prevent the transmission of HIV/AIDS. Always remember that the best choice is to use protection every time you engage in any form of sexual activity.

What happens if I find out my test is negative?

If your HIV test results are negative, remember that in the first three months after exposure to the virus you may test negative, even if you have contracted HIV. This is called the window period. Make sure you get tested again, three months after exposure, and get tested three months after each high-risk behaviour. Even if you test negative, use protection every time you are sexually active.

What happens if I find out my test is positive?

If you test positive for HIV, you will have to go for a confirmation test. If it is confirmed that you are positive, go to a counsellor at the VCTC centre or to a doctor who has experience with HIV positive people.

Do not lose hope: an HIV positive person can lead a full life with proper care and support. There are sophisticated medicines that one can take to delay the onset of AIDS. Your medical professional will talk to you about what drugs will be suitable for you and what else you can do to maintain a healthy life.

Whom should I tell if I am HIV positive? Do I have to tell anyone?

You do not have to disclose your HIV status to anyone. Not

your employer, not your parents, not your friends, no one. Your test results are completely confidential and should only be shared with you. It is up to you to tell people. But consider telling those that would be the most understanding as you will need some support over the next few years.

If you have a sexual partner, boyfriend, girlfriend, you should tell them you have HIV as soon as possible. They should go in for a test as soon as possible to find out whether they have been exposed.

What will life be like if I am HIV positive?

An HIV positive person can have a full, productive life if they take proper care of their health. At some point, you may need to take antiretroviral medications. Your doctor will prescribe antiretroviral treatment (ART), which you can get at ART centres.

Is there a cure for HIV/AIDS?

At present, there is no cure for HIV/AIDS, but with proper nutrition, hygiene and treatment, the symptoms can be controlled and you will live a long and healthy life.

Is there anywhere I can go to meet other positive people?

Seek an NGO that works with HIV positive people, or a government hospital so you can meet other people who have HIV.

Vaginal Infections/Women's Health

This section applies to all women. You do not have to be sexually active to contract any of these infections. Most are common and can be cleared up with a simple visit to the doctor and some antibiotics. There is no reason to feel embarrassed about catching these infections – they are not an indication that you have been sexually active or that you've been unhygienic. It's a good idea to confide in your mother or sister as they may have experienced it themselves and will know what to do.

Bacterial Vaginosis

What is it?

This is a bacteria that can be passed through sexual contact, although like all bacteria-based diseases it can arise by other means, like overgrowth of organisms in the vagina or from an allergic reaction.

Modes of transmission

Mostly through sexual contact or an allergic reaction.

Symptoms

Thin, smelly discharge; irritation in your genitals.

Protection

Use a condom for any sexual activity.

What should I do if I think I have it?

Go see your doctor as soon as possible.

Thrush

What is it?

Almost 75 per cent of women suffer from thrush at some point in their lives. This common infection is caused by the overpowering presence of yeast in the vagina.

Modes of transmission

Use of antibiotics or contraceptive pills; diabetes; pregnancy; wearing nylon underwear; wearing very tight, synthetic clothing; cutting out/reducing dairy products or sugar from your diet; sexual contact; sharing the washcloth that you use to clean your vagina with an infected person.

Symptoms

A lot of itching; a white, thick vaginal discharge; inflammation around the vulva.

Protection

Avoid wearing tight underwear; wear loose cotton panties and loose clothing for a while; reduce the amount of detergent you use to wash your clothes; never use a deodorant on your vagina; use pads instead of tampons during your period; eat lots of yoghurt which contains the friendly bacteria that balances out the yeast infection that causes thrush; when wiping yourself after urinating, wipe from front to back (if your poo comes in contact with your vagina, it can cause thrush and other infections).

What should I do if I think I have it?

Go see your doctor who will advise you on which over-the-counter medicines are available for thrush. These are readily available all over the country. You can confide in your mum about the infection – chances are she has had it herself and will know what to do.

Trichomoniasis (also known as trich)

What is it?

Trich is one of the most common types of parasite-based infections because it is highly contagious.

Modes of transmission

Through sexual contact.

Symptoms

Women: Foamy, yellowish, smelly discharge; some burning when you urinate, although in general, most women do not show any symptoms for the first 21 days.
Men: White discharge; some pain when urinating. But like women, most men do not show any symptoms for a long time after catching the infection.

Protection

Use condoms during sexual activity.

What should I do if I have it?

Trich is easily treated. Go see your doctor and tell them your symptoms.

Pubic Lice

What is it?

Pubic lice are small insects that look like tiny, tiny crabs. They live in the pubic hair around your genitals and in other coarse hair, like chest, underarm or eyebrow hair. The presence of lice is not an indication of how clean or dirty someone is. Although pubic lice do not live very long themselves, they lay plenty of eggs, ensuring that the infection stays on until treated.

Modes of transmission

Sexual contact; pubic lice can survive up to 24 hours without a human host so they can crawl onto other people or onto towels and sheets. So you can catch lice by sharing an infested towel or sheet or by sitting on an infected toilet seat.

Symptoms

Intense itching for both men and women.

Protection

Don't share any bedding or towels with an infected person; do not get sexually involved with an infected person as condoms will not protect you against lice.

What should I do if I have it?

There are several over-the-counter medicines available to cure lice. Go see your doctor or explain to your chemist what is going on. Do not be embarrassed – many people suffer from pubic lice and it is no indication of whether you have had sex or not. You will most likely be prescribed a medicated shampoo with which you have to wash your pubic hair as well as some disinfectant for all your sheets, towels and clothes.

Scabies

What is it?

A skin infestation which is very common all around the world.

Modes of transmission

Prolonged skin-to-skin contact; through sexual activity; or by sharing clothing, towels or bed linen with an infected person. A handshake or hug cannot spread the infection.

Symptoms

Symptoms take a while to appear (4-6 weeks) and tend to be the same for both men and women. A rash might appear on the skin, especially between the fingers, near your elbow or knee, or around the penis or breasts. This is usually accompanied by intense itching, which is very bad at night.

Protection

Avoid prolonged and sexual contact with an infected person. If you do notice the rash and itching, try and itch as little as possible as this will only worsen the infection.

What should I do if I have it?

Go and see a doctor as soon as possible. Or visit your chemist and describe your symptoms. They will give you a lotion for your body which you have to apply after showering and keep on for a few hours before washing off again. You will also need to disinfect all your bedding, clothes and towels. The itching may continue for a few weeks after treatment but no new rashes will appear 24 hours after using the lotion and disinfectant.

Cystitis/Urinary Tract Infection (UTI)

What is it?

This is an infection that affects mostly women because we have shorter urethras, so bacteria can travel into our bladders more easily. It is very common and can affect anyone of any age.

Modes of transmission

The most common way to get a UTI is from e-coli, which is the bacteria found in poo. When cleaning themselves after peeing, women can spread e-coli from their anal area to their vaginal area. You can also get a UTI from sexual activity as e-coli can also enter the system this way.

Symptoms

Painful peeing; a frequent and urgent need to pee all the time – but sometimes the pee may not even come out; cloudy urine; the need to urinate at night; lower pelvis pain.

Protection

Keep your genital area clean and remember to wipe from front to back.

Drink lots of water which will help to flush out any infections from your system.

Pee when you have to pee – try not to hold it for too long as this will give the bacteria a chance to multiply. Drinking cranberry juice can also help to prevent infection.

What should I do if I have it?

Thankfully, you do not have to live with the pain of a UTI. It is not an indication that you have had sex, as most infections have nothing to do with sexual activity, so visit your doctor and let them know you think you have a UTI. They will prescribe a course of antibiotics that will clear up the infection within a few weeks. In the meantime, take a bucket of warm water and dissolve a lot of salt in it. Wash your genital area with the bucket of salty warm water which will help with the pain and clear up the symptoms a little.

Pelvic Inflammatory Disease (PID)

What is it?

This is a broad term used to describe any type of infection that lives in the upper tract of the reproductive organs or genital area. Unfortunately, if undiagnosed and untreated, PID can lead to serious problems like infertility.

Modes of transmission

PID is commonly caused through two STDs, Chlamydia and Gonorrhoea, which are explained above. Pelvic surgery, childbirth, miscarriages or abortions carry some risk for PID as your cervix is open at this time, allowing infections to come through. The insertion of an IUD (see page 164 for more information) as a contraceptive device can also carry some risk of PID.

Symptoms

Unfortunately, the symptoms of PID do not appear for a while and are sometimes so similar to regular period pains that it is hard to detect. But here are some indications that you might have PID:

- dull pain in the lower abdomen that gets worse when you move around
- bleeding between periods or after sex
- pain during or after sex
- low energy or generally feeling unwell

- burning or pain when urinating and feeling like you can never empty your bladder
- vaginal discharge
- nausea
- lower back pain

Protection

Always, always use a condom during any sexual activity.

What should I do if I have it?

See your doctor as soon as possible. If treated quickly with a course of antibiotics and lots of rest, PID can clear up after a while. But if left untreated it can lead to long term complications with your reproductive health.

SEEING A DOCTOR

Anjali Gopalan gives you some useful advice.

How do you find a doctor you can trust?

If you engage regularly in any kind of sexual activity, you should get checked routinely by a doctor for STDs and HIV. Most women are comfortable visiting a female doctor for this. It's perfectly understandable if you do not feel like going to your family doctor. Ask a friend to recommend a doctor she/he is comfortable with. Or take a walk down your local market and see if there are any doctor's offices there. If you can afford it, consider a doctor in the private sector or look for NGOs in your area that work in sexuality and women's health. You can also visit a health care worker who can be found in a primary health centre. If none of these is available, visit the government hospital.

To ready yourself for your doctor's appointment, think about any painful or uncomfortable symptoms you might have been feeling, such as: sores, blisters, excessive vaginal discharge and itching, pain in the lower abdomen, and burning or difficulty in urinating.

If you don't have any symptoms, but your sexual partner(s) do(es), it is still important to get tested and to tell your doctor everything. It's quite possible to have an STD and not experience any symptoms. It's a good idea to ask a friend to go with you for moral support.

What's the best way to talk to your doctor about sexual activity and the fact that you are worried you may be at risk of an STD?

You might find that some doctors are more open to talking about sexual activity and will be sensitive as you explain your worries. Try and be as honest as possible. Stick to the facts.

You may say something like, 'I want to ask you about something very personal and I have heard that you are a good doctor to see about these issues. I would like to find out about STDs and HIV.' The doctor will then ask questions like whether you are sexually active, how many partners you've had and if you practised safe sex (used a condom etc.) every time.

If you are uncomfortable with any of the doctor's questions, ask her to re-phrase them. But remember that there is nothing to feel embarrassed about – it is the doctor's job to help you.

What should you do if you face judgement from a doctor about the fact that you are sexually active or at risk of an STD?

If your doctor judges you for being sexually active or for having an STD, do not accept this. Do not feel ashamed. Find another doctor who is sensitive and respectful. If a doctor or nurse in a hospital is judgemental, consider writing a letter describing what happened and post it to the senior authorities. You can also talk to counsellors at an NGO that works on women's rights. See the resources chapter for more information.

It's always a good idea to consult a doctor if you feel uneasy about something or have questions about your body or about sex. Medical professionals are trained and knowledgeable people who usually give good advice.

Nine

SEXUAL HARASSMENT AND ABUSE

Ideally, sexual activity happens between two consenting people. In other words, both individuals consciously agree to the sexual activity between them. Unfortunately, this is not always the case. Often, young women are physically touched without their consent. We call this sexual abuse. When another person touches you or makes you touch them without your consent, or without your permission, they are sexually abusing you.

What makes abuse particularly difficult to see, and thereby stop, is that it has no face. Anyone, regardless of colour, race, shape, size and gender can be abused. Likewise, abusers can also come in any shape or form – he/she could be young, old, rich, poor; a teacher, parent, priest, sibling, friend or stranger. He/she could even be a trusted and respected member of your community. In fact, in over 80 per cent of abuse cases, the victim knew their abuser well.

It's very hard to imagine that someone who is 'supposed' to love and protect you, like an uncle, a brother or a parent could do something to harm or hurt you. But the reality of abuse is that it happens close to home, behind closed doors and usually by someone you trust. Typically, an abuser uses their 'power' to intimidate, manipulate or force the victim into an abusive situation. We are taught to trust our elders, fathers, mothers, older brothers, cousins, uncles and religious leaders, so if they crawl into your bed, or watch you bathe, or ask you to touch them, we tend to believe they still have our best interests at heart, that they still care about us.

In reality, abusers are often sick people with a severe illness. In some cases, they cannot control themselves, they cannot see or choose not to see the harm they are causing. They cause havoc in innocent people's lives because of their repugnant compulsions, and they should never, ever be tolerated or trusted.

So, what should you do if you find yourself in a situation like the ones described above? What if you are being sexually abused? What if you told someone you were being abused and they didn't help you? This chapter looks at the ways in which the law can protect you and the different ways in which you can seek help. Abuse is a complex problem and it is important to remember that every individual case needs individual attention and specialized help. All the advice in this chapter is very general so as to reach out to as many people as possible, and should be read as such. We do not claim to have easy solutions to ending abusive situations but we do want you to know that you are not alone. That there are thousands of girls like you out there, and that you no longer have to suffer in silence.

We know it isn't easy to read about this, confront this, and talk about abuse. Many abusers manipulate their victims into thinking that they have done something to deserve the abuse. Or maybe the abuser explicitly threatened the victim with more violence if she tells anyone. Or the victim feels like there is no one who will understand or she worries that once people know, she will be treated differently. Or maybe she told someone about the abuse and they didn't do anything about it. Many victims pray and hope that the abuse will stop on its own if they just bide their time.

Unfortunately, the abuse will not stop until you come forward and put a stop to it. Until you tell someone who can protect you or put some physical distance between you and your abuser, or your abuser is punished for his crime. Sometimes just talking to the right person, someone who can help or offer advice or even just listen sensitively, can help you come to terms with abuse.

In the next few pages, we offer advice on how to find the right person to talk to; confide in an authority figure; report a case; seek help from a lawyer; challenge your abuser; and look for support from the many non-profit organizations which work to counter abuse. There are tips on how to tell someone you are being abused and tips on how to listen sensitively if someone tells you she/he is a victim. Whether it's someone staring at your breasts on the street, your boss looking down your top, almost getting raped by your boyfriend, or your uncle touching you in a way that makes you feel uncomfortable, a lot of you may have experienced abuse. And there is no reason to put up with it any more…

Harassment

'Why do boys tease girls?' Anju

Some boys tease because they are insecure and shy and do not know how to approach girls. So they taunt a girl from afar to get her attention.

But some people who tease are bullies. They want to see you get agitated, see you get upset. The best thing to do is to ignore them. If it ever gets to the stage where you feel unsafe or you dread seeing the people who are teasing you, you can tell someone in authority – like a teacher or the principal – that this is bothering you or you can confront them directly. Make sure you are with some friends and then say something like, 'Please leave me alone.'

Street Sexual Harassment

What Is Street Sexual Harassment?

'Why do men, irrespective of their age or relation to you, seem to check you out from top to toe?' Priya

Street sexual harassment, or eve-teasing, is the term we use when we want to talk about the harassment of a woman in a public place by a man. Almost all of us have experienced sexual harassment on the street at some point. Whether it's in the bus, while sitting in a café, walking down the street, sitting in a rickshaw in traffic or even on campus, you're stared at, brushed up against, sung to, or whistled at. No matter what you do, how you're dressed and who you're with, you can't avoid it. Eve-teasing can make you feel self-conscious, angry, frustrated and worst of all, it can eat away at your self-confidence.

How Should I Deal with It?

Some of us try to ignore the cat-calling, some of us say something back, some of us cover ourselves more when we get stared at, some of us cry in frustration and some of us lose our temper. It's up to you how to deal with it. There is no right or wrong way to deal with eve-teasing. You have to decide what works for you and you might find that each situation calls for a different reaction. The most important thing to remember is to keep yourself safe. If that means ignoring something and walking away, so be it. If it means shouting at the top of your voice for help, then do that. Here are a few general suggestions on how you can cope with sexual harassment on the street:

1. **Ignore it.** If you are alone or in a vulnerable position, the best thing to do is to focus on something straight ahead, keep your head held high and ignore the comments or lewd gestures.
2. **Say something back.** If you are with your friends and feel confident of your surroundings, you can say something back. Threaten to call the police or tell the person to leave you alone. Embarrass them into giving you an apology. You might find this is an easier option in certain cities. For example, in Kolkata or Mumbai, you will often find people

coming to your aid if you are being harassed whereas in Delhi, people tend to look the other way.

3. **File an official complaint**. If you are in university, you can complain to your professor or the head of the women's cell department (there is a women's cell in every college in the country). They will guide you as to how you can take your complaint further.
4. **Travel in groups.** Make sure you always travel with at least one friend. Ask your brother, sister or cousin to meet you outside your university gates and travel home together.
5. **Take a self-defence class.** There are several classes you can take to learn how to protect yourself, like karate, tae kwon do or judo. Not only will you figure out ways to ward off your attacker but you will feel more confident and ready for anything.
6. **Arm yourself with knowledge.** There are specific laws addressing eve-teasing, especially if it takes place in a specific context, like the home or workplace. If someone is making you feel uncomfortable or threatened, you may be able to take legal action against them.

The Law: Sexual Harassment at the Workplace

There is now a new bill in place to address any sexual harassment issues at the workplace. The law stipulates: 'No woman employee at a workplace shall be subjected to sexual harassment including unwelcome sexually determined behaviour, physical contact, advances, sexually coloured remarks, showing pornography, sexual demand, request for sexual favours or any other unwelcome conduct of sexual nature whether verbal, textual, physical, graphic or electronic or by any other actions...'

If anyone says or does anything that makes you feel uncomfortable, you are well within your rights to have them removed from your workplace. For example, if your colleague shows you a pornographic email or your boss makes a joke about women or someone comments on the clothes you are wearing or if anyone deliberately brushes past you, as well as any other behaviour that makes you feel uncomfortable, then this Bill will help protect you. If you find yourself in a situation like the ones outlined above, lodge a complaint with the HR department or your boss. Then consult a lawyer or an organization like Sakshi (see resources), which helps women fight sexual harassment at the workplace. For more information on this law and others working for women's rights in India, visit http://wcd.nic.in.

Ragging

Ragging is the term used to describe the ill-treatment of freshmen by their seniors. Rampant across the country and in all types of educational institutions, ragging is more common among boys but incidents with girls are on the increase.

In 2001, the Supreme Court ruled that ragging is illegal and includes, 'Any disorderly conduct whether by words spoken, or written, or by an act with the effect of teasing, treating or handling with rudeness any other student; indulging in rowdy or indisciplined activities which cause or are likely to cause annoyance, hardship or psychological harm or to raise fear or apprehension thereof, in a fresher or a junior student, or asking the students to do any act or perform something which such student will not do in the ordinary course and which has the effect of causing or generating a sense of shame or embarrassment so as to adversely affect the physique or psyche of a fresher or a junior student.'

Most commonly, juniors are expected to clean, carry errands and 'work' for their seniors but this soon extends to harsh and torturous treatment of the junior. Many girls have been made to strip, perform sexual acts, talk about their parents in a sexual way or touch themselves in front of other people. The consequences of such behaviour can have long-lasting mental, physical and emotional effects on young women.

What Do I Do if I am being Ragged?

Ragging is not something you have to put up with. Seek help straightaway. Tell someone in authority, like a professor or even the principal about what's happening to you. Or tell your parents and ask them to take you out of college until the matter is resolved or help you find alternate living arrangements. At the end of this book, you will find a resources section, which includes the contact details of several organizations working to combat ragging on campuses. Some of them even offer online counselling and legal advice.

Abuse

What is abuse?

Abuse is when another human being – your partner, friend, brother, father, sister, mother, grandparent, a stranger, anyone – uses force over you. Abuse is usually divided into three categories – physical abuse, emotional abuse and sexual abuse, but many victims are usually subjected to all types of abuse so these categories should only be used as a guideline. If anyone makes you feel threatened or scared, whether physically, emotionally or sexually, you are most likely a victim of abuse.

Physical Abuse

If someone hits, kicks, strangles, pushes, pulls, throws things at you, spits on you or harms you in any physical way, they are physically abusing you. You do not have to be slapped or kicked consistently for it to mean that you are being abused. It can happen just once to make you feel threatened and scared.

Emotional Abuse

If someone constantly criticizes you or puts you down, intimidates you, ignores you, controls your every move, prevents you from meeting your friends or family, or threatens you, they are emotionally abusive. Some of us may not even realize that we are being emotionally abused because we are manipulated into thinking we have done something to deserve the treatment we receive. An abuser can slowly eat away at your self-esteem and confidence until you do not even question why you are treated in a certain way but simply accept it.

Dowry Harassment

Although the practice of dowry was outlawed in the early 1960s many families continue to demand a dowry from their daughter-in-law's family. A woman may be subjected to physical and mental torture so that her in-laws can squeeze more money out of her family or because they are not happy with what they got in the dowry. In some cases, a woman may even be killed by her husband's family. The National Crime Records Bureau recorded a dowry death every 77 minutes in 2005 but some sources estimate the figure to be even higher, closer to 25,000 dowry deaths a year.

What Do I Do if I Think I am Being Abused or Harassed?

The box below provides information on what you can do if you are being physically, emotionally or sexually abused. Also, Chapter 10 lists organizations that you can contact if you need help with a legal case, need protection or if you just need someone to talk to.

The Law: Domestic Violence/Dowry Harassment

In 2006, the Indian government introduced The Protection Of Women From Domestic Violence Act 2005, which also covers dowry harassment. Under this Act, domestic violence is defined as:

- habitual assault on a person
- the intention to make someone's life miserable using either physical or emotional pressure
- forcing the victim to live an immoral life
- harming the victim in any way

However, a man can argue that he has hurt a woman in order to protect himself or his property.

Although the Act mainly protects wives and female live-in partners from their husband or partner, it also offers protection to sisters, widows, mothers from an abusive male and/or his relatives.

Under this Act, you are entitled to protection from your abuser – he is not allowed to contact, follow or try and see you. You are also entitled to secure housing, which can include the home you shared with your husband/partner/joint family even if you do not own it.

Most importantly, the law covers not just physical abuse but the threat of abuse, whether it is physical, sexual, emotional or financial. So, if someone threatens or tortures a woman about dowry, they could be prosecuted under this aspect of the Act.

Sexual Abuse

What Is Sexual Abuse?

Sexual abuse is when someone touches you or asks you to touch them without your consent and in a way that makes you feel uncomfortable. You do not have to be raped or even be touched on your genitals for you to feel violated. For example, if someone hugs you, kisses you, touches your breasts, asks you to touch any part of their body, touches your genitals, makes you touch their genitals, rubs up against you, makes you take a bath in front of them, forces you to look at pornographic material, takes revealing pictures of you without your permission, follows you home and stalks you, washes your body, makes you wash their body, or lies next to you naked, this is considered sexual abuse.

What Is Incest?

Incest is when someone you are related to, like your brother, uncle, father, grandfather, touches you or makes you touch them in a sexual way.

Who Are the Abusers?

The abusers can be anyone and from anywhere. Someone within your family, a worker, a stranger, a friend or even a boyfriend can abuse you. Rich, old, young, male or female, abusers come in all shapes and sizes so it's impossible to know who is an abuser just by looking at them.

What Should I Do If I am Abused?

You need to tell someone what's happened to you. Maybe a friend? Or a teacher you like? Or if you have a university counsellor, tell her? Confide in your mother or your sister or maybe even a cousin. Talking about what's happened to you, saying the words out loud and having an empathetic listener will help you deal with the abuse. You do not have to go through this alone.

If you find you just can't face the thought of telling anyone or you don't trust anybody, try writing it down. Put down everything that's in your mind on a piece of paper. It doesn't have to make sense and no one has to see it. But letting all your emotions out in one go will help you deal with your situation.

I would really love to say that you should go to the police straightaway and get the molester arrested. But the truth is that the experience of going to a police station is intimidating and scary and filing a complaint may not even get you anywhere. Having said that, if more of us muster the courage to come out in the open and talk about what's happening, the easier it will be for our younger sisters, friends and daughters to prosecute their abusers. But when you have been abused, the only thing you need to worry about is *yourself*, not about making a political statement or making the world a better place for the next generation. Just do what feels right for you.

There are no easy solutions to the pain, heartache and sadness that you may feel as a result of being abused. Although talking will help you come to terms with what happened and support from loved ones will make things a little easier, there is no quick-fix solution to feeling better. Give yourself time to heal. Most importantly, remember that you are in no way to blame. You did nothing to provoke him, you didn't wear the wrong clothes or smile too often. You didn't deserve this. Never blame yourself.

'What do I do if I tell my mother about some uncle who touched me on my private parts and she feels helpless? She says she is not in a position to say anything.' Shashi

Unfortunately, a lot of people, like your mother, shy away from the topic of sexual abuse and are either too embarrassed or too scared to talk about it openly, even if the person being hurt is someone they love. Sometimes they are worried about upsetting the abuser, who could be a family member or someone considered important in society, or they could be scared, uncertain about how to react or whom to ask for help.

But please don't give up. You were right to confide in someone – not only to help you heal and talk about what you have been through but also to stop your uncle from touching you again. Please tell someone else. Maybe your friend? Or your father? Whoever you feel closest to and someone who might be more receptive. In the meantime, try and avoid spending time alone with your uncle. Remember that your uncle touching you is not your fault and nobody has the right to abuse their position of power in a way that makes you feel uncomfortable.

Open Ears, Open Minds

Elaan, a non-profit organization working to counter sexual abuse in India offers advice on how to listen sensitively when someone confides in you about being abused.

If someone has confided in you, remember that it takes a lot of courage to come forward and talk about what's happening. So, if your friend, daughter, sister, granddaughter, cousin or niece tells you that she is being abused, you need to take it very seriously. Here are a few suggestions on how you can handle the situation calmly and sensitively.

1 **Listen.** It is important to be attentive to what the victim is saying, and not to ask too many questions or interrupt them. The victim might feel cornered or interrogated if asked too many questions. They should be allowed to speak at their own pace, and be silent if they so wish. They should never be hurried or forced into talking.

2 **Believe the victim.** It is important not only to believe the survivor, but also to tell him/her that you do, in fact, believe what they are saying. Talking about it was an extremely difficult step for them to take, and assuring them that you believe them will boost their confidence and sense of security ten-fold.

3 **Avoid displaying too much emotion.** Showing any kind of shock or horror at what the victim reveals is a complete no-no, as it only serves to reinforce their sense of guilt and shame. It is important to keep a grip on one's feelings instead of being carried away by rage or grief.

4 **Commend the victim for being brave.** You should acknowledge the trust that the victim has placed in you by confessing to you. The victim needs to be told that he/she was correct and courageous to come forward.

5 **Don't make promises you can't keep.** Often, the first instinct after listening to a victim disclose the abuse, is to promise him/her that he/she will be protected from further harm. However, in many cases, this is nearly impossible to do, especially if the perpetrator is a parent, a close relative or a trusted family friend. Many times, there is not enough evidence to prove the sexual abuse, and thus it becomes impossible to even remove the survivor from the toxic environment he/she is trapped in. However, it is important to assure the victim that there is at least one adult that he/she can trust.

6 **Tell the victim that he/she is not at fault.** Assuring a victim that he/she is in no way responsible for what happened to him/her, is extremely beneficial for the

tormented person and can go a long way in easing the guilt that a victim of abuse is bound to feel.

7 **Never tell the victim what to do.** Unless the victim categorically asks to be told what to do, one should never impose one's own ideas about how the situation is to be handled, no matter how correct the plan of action might be. The victim needs to feel that his/her opinion counts and nothing should be done if the victim does not want it. Instead, it is more feasible to ask the survivor if he/she is comfortable with taking action.

8 **Don't judge the offender in front of the victim.** Since, more often than not, the abuser is someone whom the victim is close to, he/she tends to have conflicting feelings towards that person. The victim might love the person, but not like what he/she is doing to them. In such a case, openly condemning the offender in front of the victim might backfire, and the victim might resort to defending the offender, out of the love that the victim has for him/her.

9 **Let the victim know that he/she is not alone.** It is imperative to convince the victim that he/she is not alone and isolated, that there are other people who have gone through the same thing and understand how it feels. Knowing that he/she is not the only one who has gone through the painful experience may lift a weight off the victim's chest and help them deal with their trauma.

The tables on the next two pages outline both negative and positive body language and verbal responses to help you respond to the situation.

Body Language

POSITIVE	NEGATIVE
Appearing alert and attentive	Seeming distracted and restless
Displaying empathy (*not* pity)	Sympathizing too much, thereby making the victim/ survivor feel inferior
Showing support through body language, rather than employing touch	Overtly displaying affection in an attempt to pacify the victim
Remaining objective without appearing detached	Becoming overtly emotional
Creating a comfort level	Being cold/formal
Giving the survivor his/her time and space	Interrupting and/or hastening the disclosure

Verbal Response

POSITIVE	NEGATIVE
It was brave of you to tell someone.	Why did you wait so long to tell someone?
Sexual abuse is a crime.	Thank god it wasn't rape!

Sexual abuse is *not* normal, even if the perpetrator is of the opposite sex.	It is a normal experience and had to happen some time.
Sexual abuse is *never* the victim's fault.	Maybe it was something you were wearing.
I will not judge you.	Now you are impure!

Sexual Abuse/Harassment/Eve-teasing: the Law

In 1997, sexual harassment laws were put into place and sexual harassment was defined as an 'unwelcome sexual gesture or behaviour whether indirectly or directly'. This includes 'sexually-coloured remarks, physical contact and advances, showing pornography, demand for sexual favours, or any other unwelcome physical, verbal/nonverbal conduct being sexual in nature'.

Provisions of the Indian Penal Code include cases where the accused sexually harasses or insults the modesty of a woman by way of either obscene acts or songs or by means of words, gesture or acts intended to insult the modesty of a woman; and such a person is punishable by the law.

It is worth noting that under Section 294 of the Indian Penal Code that deals with sexual harassment, the 'obscene act or song' has to be performed in front of other people. That means if you are alone, there is no way you can prove what happened. If you find yourself in a situation where you are alone and someone sings, talks or exposes himself to you, try and use your mobile phone to take a picture or record a short video. This will give you much-needed evidence.

Rape

What Is Rape?

Rape is when someone uses force, violence, or emotional pressure to have sex with you without your consent. Having sex with someone who is physically challenged, drunk, asleep, or unable to give consent because they are mentally ill or drugged, is also considered rape. Rape is a crime even if the attacker and victim know one another. You have the right to say no to sex at any time, even in the middle of a sexual encounter.

Rape Within a Relationship

In most cases, the attacker and victim will know one another. The attacker might be a family friend or a teacher or your boss or your friend or your colleague or even your boyfriend. Rape is when someone forces or pressures you into a sexual encounter that you do not want to engage in. Which means that if you and your boyfriend are fooling around and touching one another and he wants to go further and you say no, he has to stop. If he carries on pressuring you, physically forcing you or even emotionally manipulating you into going further when you have said no or pushed him away or basically haven't said yes, then this is considered rape.

When someone you have previously trusted, like a boyfriend, family friend or teacher, abuses your trust, it can be hurtful and confusing. You might even find that you are blaming yourself.

Maybe you think you led him on? Or maybe it's okay that he expected to have sex if you were kissing? Or maybe you put your hands down his pants and made him think it was okay to do the same to you? Or maybe you think no one will believe you? If you find yourself asking these sorts of questions, you have to remind yourself that nothing you did before the attack matters. If at any point:

you asked him to stop
said you didn't want to have sex
pushed him away
fell asleep
didn't say yes

then he should have stopped. It's never okay, even if you are in a relationship with someone, to pressure anyone into doing anything. Healthy, safe relationships are built on respect and whoever you are with should listen to your needs and desires and respect you.

If you find yourself in a situation where your boyfriend/husband has raped you or coerced you into a sexual act against your will, don't be afraid to break off the relationship. In fact, it's the safest and wisest decision you could make. Get as far away as possible from this person. You are not safe with them.

What Is Date Rape?

Date rape is when you may have gone on a date consensually with someone but during the date or after it, they have used violence and force to have sex with you. This kind of rape usually involves some kind of drug which is slipped into a girl's drink which knocks her unconscious.

What Should You Do if You are Raped?

There are very clear laws prohibiting rape in India and so it is easier to prosecute than for sexual abuse incidents. Nevertheless, it is not an easy process so you have to be prepared to face lots of questions about yourself and about what happened. I am not saying this to discourage you from reporting your rape. But it's important to understand and be prepared for the process of filing for a claim.

Try not to shower or wash your body straightaway. Don't throw away the clothes you were wearing when it happened. Then go to a hospital. Tell them what happened. They will administer a rape test, which means they will examine your body and collect any residue left by your attacker. Usually, the hospital will call the police if you say it's okay to do so and you might be asked a few questions. According to protocol, the police should then build up a case and arrest the person who attacked you once they have the evidence.

I wish I could say it is going to be an easy process but the truth is that reporting a rape is not a straightforward matter. The police can be intimidating, intrusive or dismissive. All kinds of people, from your family to the medical personnel, can show a lack of insensitivity that is shocking and painful. That is why only 1 rape out of every 53 is reported. And of the rape cases that are reported, only a very small percentage result in convictions.

Again, like sexual abuse, talking about rape and your experience will help you deal with it. Talking can be really therapeutic. Some of us have a tendency to bury the pain or to deal with it alone but this only leads to more sadness and grief. Sharing the burden with someone, like your mother, sister, friend or cousin will help you come to terms with your trauma. There is no reason why you should suffer in silence.

At the end of this book, you will find a list of websites and crisis centres that run counselling services. Try getting in touch with one of these organizations and talk to them about how you feel. They are sympathetic, kind people who can help you through some of the heartache. You do not have to go through this alone. Also, you can write to us at info@bodytalkindia.com if you just feel like talking or visit www.bodytalkindia.com for more information.

'Why does rape happen?' Aekta

There are many theories out there about why men rape women. Some people believe that rape is ultimately about one person asserting their power over another. In other words, using physical and mental force to get what they want. Others believe that it has something to do with the way women are perceived in the world – we are often seen as the property of men, as lesser beings that are here to serve men and do what they want. In reality, both theories are true and can help explain why men rape women.

Most importantly, remember what rape is *not* about. Rape is never about desire, rape is never about what the girl was wearing or whether she slept with other people before or whether she didn't put up a 'good fight'. These are unjust accusations designed to make the victim feel responsible for what happened to her and hold no truth whatsoever.

Protecting Yourself

'How can a girl save herself from getting raped?' Sweta

Every girl and woman is a potential rape victim. It can happen anywhere, at any time. Here are a few rules to keep you as safe as possible:

1. Eighty-five per cent of rape victims know their attacker. If you feel threatened by someone, even if you know and usually trust them, please, please tell someone and get away from them as soon as possible. Lock yourself in a room or leave the house at once.
2. If you are dating, make sure you meet your date or friend in a public place. No matter how well the first or second date is going, don't agree to go back to his house or anywhere else.
3. Always make sure you have a mobile phone with you. Make sure it is charged and working. You never know when you are going to need it.
4. Trust your instincts. If something feels or sounds dodgy, chances are it is.
5. Carry a travel-size deodorant in your bag. If someone attacks you, try and spray it into their face, aiming for the eyes. This might buy you some time to get away. But only do this if

you feel relatively sure you can escape. Do not attempt this if he has a knife or gun.

6. Take a self-defence class. Learn how to kick ass. Make sure you are in shape so that if you do need to run, you can!
7. Walk confidently and always look like you know where you are. People are more likely to attack someone who looks vulnerable and scared.
8. Make it clear how far you want to go with someone. And remember that it's okay to say no and stop at any time. Speak up and say *no*.

'If a friend almost suffers date rape with a guy she really, really liked is it okay for her to forgive him later and get into a relationship with him? He is supposed to be very nice. But how can we know that he won't repeat this?' Maya

When something traumatic happens to us, like we are almost raped by someone, it's very common to want to forget that it happened or to imagine that that's not what really happened. You might even feel an emotional connection with your attacker. This happens because the attacker might make you feel like you deserved it or didn't fight back 'hard enough'. These are, of course, all lies meant to make you feel scared and disempowered.

Your friend should not enter into a relationship with this boy. There is a very good chance that he will try to rape her again and will never offer her the respect and personal freedom she deserves. It is not okay or acceptable for someone to try and rape you. He is clearly not a 'good' person. My advice is to get away from him as quickly as possible and to tell someone in a position of authority about what happened. Tell your friend to speak to a counsellor or check out one of the online counselling services listed in the resources chapter at the end of this book. Rape does not have to actually occur for someone to feel violated and abused.

The Law: Sexual Violence

Under the Indian Penal Code, a rape has been committed under the following circumstances:

1. Sexual intercourse against the victim's will.
2. Without the victim's consent.
3. With her consent, when her consent has been obtained by putting her or any person that she may be interested in fear of death or hurt.
4. With her consent, when the man knows that he is not her husband.
5. With her consent, when at the time of giving such consent she is intoxicated, or suffering from unsoundness of mind and does not understand the nature and consequences of that to which she gives consent.
6. With or without her consent when she is under 16 years of age.

If you have been raped, you are within your rights to persecute your attacker. See Chapter 10 for more information on whom you can contact to help you fight your case.

Ten | Resources

This chapter tries to cover all the different aspects of this book – from relationships to depression to HIV to rape to suicide to eating disorders to being gay – and gives you as much information as possible on websites, helplines, organizations and books that can help you overcome whatever problems you might be facing or any questions you might have.

Calling Helplines: A Note

The people who answer your calls are trained to be as sensitive and understanding as possible so you can be open and honest about what's bothering you. They may have some useful advice or simply listen to you. But don't give away personal information to anyone on the phone, like your address, email or phone number. If you don't feel comfortable at any time, just put the phone down.

Acne

An online support group for acne sufferers. Includes tips, treatments and sensible advice.
Website: www.stopspots.org

Self-Esteem

The La Belle Foundation has been helping to build self-esteem and teaching people to value themselves since 1980. Click on the tab towards the left of the page that says Curriculum, then choose from one of the options – Personality, Performance or Presentation – to find a list of questions that will encourage you to explore yourself and help you work on your self-esteem.
Website: www.selfesteem.org

Body Image

A great site committed to helping women feel good about their bodies is www.bodypositive.com. Their motto is Change Your Mind, Change Your Culture, and Let Your Body Be.

About-Face encourages readers to challenge the media and pop culture and the messages they send to young women. Each week, they pick a mainstream company and ask them why they choose certain images in their advertising campaigns.
Website: www.about-face.org

Eating Disorders

An online resource that believes that eating disorders are a sign of something deeper is www.something-fishy.org

A site designed to help young people cope with eating disorders is www.b-eat.co.uk/YoungPeople/Home

Depression

Delhi

Snehi is a Delhi-based non-profit organization that is concerned with mental health issues and runs a helpline.
Tel: 011-6597 8181
Timings: 2 p.m. to 7 p.m. every day
Website: www.snehi.org
Email: info@snehi.org or snehi.india@gmail.com

Swanchetan is a 'non-profit, non-governmental, apolitical and secular organization that provides psychological help and support to victims of violence, abuse and trauma'. They run a 24-hour helpline for women in distress.
Tel: 011-26123931/ 26135296/ 9810262767
Website: www.swanchetan.org
Email: info@swanchetan.org

Sanjeevani Society for Mental Health offers counselling to young women.
Tel: 2686 2222/ 2686 4488

Befrienders is an online service that offers information on depression and suicide.
Website: www.befrienders.org

Chennai

Sneha
Address: No.7, Avvai Shanmugam Lane, Royapettah, Chennai - 600 014

Tel: 044-28115050

Timings: 8 a.m. to 10 p.m. every day

Email: sneha_ft@vsnl.net

New Delhi

Sumaitri

Address: NDMC Complex, 48 Babar Road,
New Delhi - 110 001

Tel: 011-3710763

Timings: 2 p.m. to 10 p.m. every day

Mumbai

Samaritans-Sahara

Address: 1st floor, Seva Niketan, Sir JJ Road, Byculla,
Mumbai - 400 008

Tel: 022-23073451

Timings: 3 p.m. to 9 p.m. on weekdays,
10 a.m. to 9 p.m. on weekends

Email: smaritns@vsnl.com

Pondicherry

Maitreyi

Address: 225, Thiagumudali Street,
Pondicherry - 615 001

Tel: 0413 - 2339999

Timings: 2 p.m. to 8 p.m. every day

Email: bimaitreyi@rediffmail.com

Kochi

Maithri

Address: Vimalalayam Building, Ashirbhavan Road, Kacherippady, Kochi - 682 018

Tel: 0484-2396272

Timings: 10 a.m. to 8 p.m. every day

Navi Mumbai

Aasra

Address: A4, Plot 43, Tanwar View Chs, Sector 7, Koparkhairane, Navi Mumbai - 400709

Tel: 022-27546669

Timings: 3 p.m. to 9 p.m. every day

Email: aasrahelpline@yahoo.com

Ahmedabad

Saath

Address: B-12 Nilamber Complex, H.L Commerce, College Road, Ahmedabad - 380 009

Tel: 079-6305544

Timings: 1 p.m. to 7 p.m. every day

Email: saakul@wilnetonline.net

Secunderabad

Roshni

Address: 70, Paigah Colony, Behind Anand Theatre, Sardar Patel Road, Secunderabad - 500 003

Tel: 040-7904646/7902322

Timings: 10 a.m. to 2 p.m. and 4 p.m. to 8 p.m.
from Monday to Saturday
Email: bi_roshni@yahoo.com

Kolkata

Lifeline
Address: P.O Box 9455, Kolkata - 700 016
Tel: 033-24745255/ 24745886
Email: lifefoun@cal.vsnl.net.in

The Royal College of Psychiatrists has a useful guide on depression, available in Bengali, English and Urdu. Check out the menu on the left side of the screen for more information on depression.
Website: www.rcpsych.ac.uk

Gender

Prajaak, a Kolkata-based organization works with young people on issues like gender identity, self-esteem and empowerment.
Tel: 033-24000455
Email: contact@praajak.org or frontdesk@praajak.org
Website: www.praajak.org

Buying Condoms Online

You will need a credit card and have to spend over Rs 150 but you can buy condoms online at either www.kamasutraontheweb.com or www.moodsplanet.com

Sexual and Reproductive Health

Tarshi (Talking About Reproductive and Sexual Health Issues) runs a Hindi and English helpline particularly for women.
Tel: 011-2437 2229
Timings: 10 a.m. to 4 p.m. from Monday to Wednesday

India Aids Project offers some great quizzes and easy to read information on STDs, safe sex and counselling.
Website: www.indiaids.org

Scarleteen is a comprehensive, non judgmental, non patronizing website that offers tons of information and advice on everything from your body to sex to relationships.
Website: www.scarleteen.com

Abortion

Abortion Services

Parivar Seva Sanstha is an organization that aims to provide affordable reproductive health services, including abortion, in 21 Indian states. For a full list of their clinics, visit www.parivarseva.org

Emotional Support

You can talk to other women who have undergone abortions at www.afterabortion.com

Exhale, a US-based free counselling service for women who have undergone abortions.
Tel: 00 1-866-439-4253
Website: www.4exhale.org

Another free US-based counselling service that also helps with adoption worries and related pregnancy issues can be found at www.yourbackline.org
Tel: 00 1-888-493-0092

For some simple ideas to help you through the emotional lows after abortion check out www.peaceafterabortion.com

Gay and Lesbian

Sappho
Founded in 1999, Sappho is a support group for lesbian, bisexual and transgender women. They offer confidential counselling and have a resource centre, Chetana, which is open to members of the public.

You can write them a letter, email or call their helpline for confidential support and help.
Address: 11A, Jogendra Gardens (South) Ground Floor, (Near Hindol Park), Kolkata – 700 078
Tel: 098315 18320
Timings: 10 a.m. to 9 p.m. every day
Website: www.sapphokolkata.org
Email: sappho1999@rediffmail.com or sappho1999@gmail.com

Trikone is a south-Asian specific gay and lesbian online forum/ magazine. A free excerpt from the magazine is available online every month.
Website: www.trikone.org

Sangini Helpline is for women who are attracted to women.
Tel: 011 6567-6450
Timings: 12 p.m. to 3 p.m. Tuesday, 6 p.m. to 8 p.m. on Friday

Naz Dost Helpline is for men who are attracted to men.
Tel: 011-2981 2287
Timings: 1 p.m. to 7 p.m. from Monday to Saturday

PFLAG is a support group for parents, families and friends of lesbians, gays and transgender people.
Website: www.pflag.org

The Nigah Queer Collective aims to promote awareness and tolerance of the gay and lesbian community through events and workshops.
Website: www.nigahdelhi.blogspot.com

HIV/STDS

Naz Foundation

This non-profit organization works to educate people about HIV, provide counselling and testing facilities to those at risk from HIV.
Tel: 011-26910499
Website: www.nazindia.org
Email naz@airtelmail.in or naz@nazindia.org

Y.R. Gaitonde Centre for AIDS Research and Education (YRG CARE)

This non-profit organization is based in Chennai and offers services like counselling, treatment, testing and prevention. They offer pre-test, post-test counselling as well as testing facilities and will charge you according to what you can afford. They also run one of the only inpatient and outpatient HIV clinics in the country.
Helpline: 044-2254 2254

Hotline: 98400 69000

Testing Facility: YRGC, VHS Campus,
Rajiv Gandhi Road, Taramani, Chennai – 600113

Tel: 044-22542929

Timings: 9 a.m. to 4 p.m. from Monday to Saturday

Website: www.yrgcare.org

Email: info@yrgcare.org

Heroes Project India is a government-funded initiative to raise awareness and reduce the stigma around HIV. You can call one of their helplines (which are managed by Population Services International (PSI)) or sms AIDS to 2525 or sms ASK to 7827 for information on HIV/AIDS.

Tel:

Delhi: 011-24372229

Timing: 10 a.m. to 4 p.m. from Monday to Wednesday

Mumbai: 022-2389 2222

Chennai: 044-25345555

Vizag: 0891-2552222

Website: www.heroesprojectindia.org

The Body is a complete HIV/AIDS Resource. This site has all the information and facts without any of the morality judgements. Click on the prevention tab to the right of the page for some great, frequently asked questions and non-squeamish advice.

Website: www.thebody.com

National Aids Control Organization (NACO) is a government organization which runs several helplines and has a useful website informing you of your rights if you are

HIV positive. They also have 350 community centres around the country which provide support, outreach, treatment and counselling to those with HIV.
Website: www.nacoonline.org

Lawyers Collective HIV/AIDS Unit. If you have been subjected to any kind of discrimination – whether it was obstruction to treatment or you were tested without your permission or your right to confidentiality was breached – the Lawyers Collective can help you fight your case. And if you are worried about your HIV status becoming public by taking it to court, you can fight the case under another name.
Mumbai:
Tel: 022-22875482/3
Email: aidslaw@lawyerscollective.org
New Delhi:
Tel: 011-24377101/2
Email: aidslaw1@lawyerscollective.org
Bangalore:
Tel: 080-41239130/1
Email: aidslaw2@lawyerscollective.org
Website: www.lawyerscollective.org

Positively Women is a helpline answered by HIV positive women based in the UK.
Tel: +44 20 7713 0222
Website: www.positivelywomen.org.uk

For more information on HIV and AIDS, visit www.condomessentialwear.co.uk, www.ssha.info (Society of Sexual Health Advisers), www.avert.org or www.aidsmap.com.

Sexual Harassment/Abuse

Tulir is a centre for the prevention and healing of child abuse.
Address: J Block, Old no. 33 New no. 18, 7th Street,
Anana Nagar East, Chennai - 600 102
Tel: 26192026 / 26190771.
Email: tulircphcsa@yahoo.co.in
Blog: www.childsexualabuseinindia.blogspot.com

Elaan is an organization formed by child abuse survivors to help combat sexual abuse.
Address: IB 150 Sector III, Bidhannagar, Salt Lake,
Kolkata - 700 091
Tel: +91 98741 35977 / 033 6454 4564
Email: elaanspeak@yahoo.co.in. For a one-on-one consultation with Pranaadhika please email anna.chronism@gmail.com.
Blog: www.aboutabuse.blogspot.com. They also have facebook, orkut and my space accounts.

Project OBO: Our Bodies, (Our) Opinions is a Kolkata-based non-profit organization made up primarily of university students who work with young people to address gender stereotypes, sexual development and abuse through the use of conversation and art.
Address: Project OBO: Our Bodies, (Our) Opinions,
c/o Mirna Guha,
5B Pushpa Apartments, 63A Bright Street,
Kolkata-700019, West Bengal, India
Tel: 098310 72971
Email: projectobo.2009@gmail.com

Rahi is a support centre for survivors of child sexual abuse, particularly incest. They have some useful information on what to do if you or someone you love has been abused. You can also contact them with specific problems and questions.
Tel: 011-26238466/ 26224042/ 26227647
Email: counsellor@rahifoundation.org

Breakthrough is an organization that uses popular culture to advance women's rights. 232
Website: www.breakthrough.tv

TEAR is an online resource for people who are being abused who need friendly advice.
Website: www.teensagainstabuse.org

Dancing in the Dark is a wonderful resource that encourages you to share your sexual abuse survival story.
Website: www.dancinginthedarkness.com

RAINN
After she was raped, Tori Amos co-founded this organization which helps survivors of rape, incest and sexual abuse deal with what happened to them.
Website: www.rainn.org
They also offer immediate counselling online.
Timings: 12 p.m. to 12 a.m. US Eastern Time (which is 10.5 hours behind Delhi time) from Monday to Friday.
Website: online.rainn.org

Bitter chocolate by Pinki Virani tells a personal story of sexual abuse.

Street Sexual Harassment/Eve-Teasing

Jagori is an organization that is campaigning to make Delhi a safer place for women. They have lots of free booklets on how to look after yourself and run a helpline for women facing harassment on the street.

Address: B-114, Shivalik, Malviya Nagar,
New Delhi
Tel: 011-2669 2700 .
Email: safedelhi@jagori.org

The **DTC** (Delhi Transport Commission) has installed two 24-hour helplines to help women lodge complaints and seek help about harassment on buses.
Tel: 52555 (toll free) or 9971755555.

The Delhi Commission for Women
You can reach them through one of their helplines 011- 23379181/23370597. They also have a 24 hour rape crisis line – 011-23370557.
Website: www.delhi.gov.in/wps/wcm/connect/Lib_DCW/dcw/home

The Blank Noise Project is a blog dedicated to sharing stories of being harassed on the street, the workplace, in college or anywhere.
Website: www.blanknoiseproject.blogspot.com

Ragging

CURE, the Coalition to Uproot Ragging in Education, is dedicated to raising awareness about and eliminating the mental,

psychological and physical torture juniors undergo at the hands of their seniors. They have a special section for girls who are being ragged.
Email: girls@noragging.com

They also offer counselling services through a licensed psychologist.
Email: You can contact him directly at vikas_msharma@noragging.com or write to the Patheya Counselling services in Mumbai at patheya@rediffmail.com. Or you can email them at cure@noragging.com
Website: They have an extensive website, www.noragging.com, which is packed with information, possible solutions to ragging and the latest news.
Blog: noragging.blogspot.com

SAVE or Society Against Violence in Education, runs a website that allows victims to share their stories and seek help from one another. They also try to help individual victims with medical and physiological advice but their resources are limited.
Website: www.no2ragging.org
Email: contact@no2ragging.org or help@no2ragging.org

Sexual Harrassment at the Workplace

Sakshi is an organization that offers legal advice to women who are facing sexual harassment at the workplace.
Email: sakshipaths@yahoo.com

About the Contributors

Anjali Gopalan is the Founder and Executive Director of the Naz Foundation (India) Trust, a Delhi-based NGO dedicated to fighting HIV/AIDS. In 2000, Anjali opened the Naz Care Home, a safe and supportive environment that houses 44 HIV-positive children between the ages of 18 months and 16 years.

As an advocate for the rights of the LGBT (Lesbian, Gay, Bisexual and Transgender) community, Anjali spearheaded the eight-year legal battle against Section 377 of the Indian Penal Code, which culminated in the historic judgment decriminalizing homosexuality and the infringement on individual rights in 2009.

In 2001, Anjali was awarded the Commonwealth Award for her work with marginalized communities. The Manava Seva Dharma Samvardhani presented her the Sadguru Gnanananda Award in 2003 for supporting those living with HIV/AIDS. In 2005, she was shortlisted for the Nobel Peace Prize in recognition of her work to bring harmony to those whose lives have none.

In March 2007, Anjali was honoured as a Woman Achiever by the Ministry of Women and Child Development. She became an Ashoka Fellow in recognition of her achievements as a social entrepreneur in 2007.

Monica Mody practises her writing and teaching as a feminist and queer activist citizen. She has worked with Breakthrough India and with the Centre for Feminist Legal Research, New Delhi, as a rights advocate for women's, queer, and free speech issues. She was a member of the Nigah queer collective and has led events and workshops on gender and sexuality with young people. She is a non-practising lawyer and is currently pursuing an MFA in poetry at the University of Notre Dame.

Pranaadhika Sinha Devburman is an artist and social entrepreneur based in Kolkata, West Bengal. She founded the NGO, Elaan-Combat Child Sexual Abuse, in 2001 while she was a student at the Calcutta International School. She is currently involved with creating human rights awareness through digital media such as video-blogging under the WAVE programme (Women Aloud-Video Blogging for Empowerment, a MacCarthur Foundation supported initiative). She is also in the process of setting up an initiative, which will reach out to 'Middle India' as part of an endeavor to educate, empower and involve them in the social development process. This idea has been inspired in part by the Tata Jagriti Yatra for which she was a facilitator in 2009-10 (www.jagritiyatra.com). When not working, she designs and builds furniture, takes care of her tattoo studio and travels around India.

Mirna Guha is a 23-year-old Master's student of English literature at Jadavpur University, Kolkata. She is also a musician, independent researcher, and dedicated to social change. She worked at Elaan, an organization working towards child sexual abuse awareness and prevention in Kolkata, as a facilitator and peer counsellor. Mirna also freelanced as a facilitator for human/child rights workshops, where she worked with over a hundred young people, disseminating information about rights, responsibilities and self-development.

In February 2009, she was awarded the Lattoo Fellowship to implement Project OBO: Our Bodies, (Our) Opinions, an initiative that uses art and conversation to raise awareness among adolescents about issues like gender, stereotypes, and sexual abuse. Besides working towards breaking taboos and creating positive spaces for young people to thrive in, Mirna is extremely passionate about all forms of performance art.

Acknowledgements

Thank you to:
All the young women who participated in the workshops and without whom this book wouldn't have been possible, in particular Shruti and Hemani.

The professors and principals at IP College, Kamala Nehru, Miranda House, Delhi School of Economics, DU, Apeejay Institute of Management, and Jadavpur University, especially Nitoo Das and Nidhi Bhandari.

Much, much gratitude to:

Monica Mody
Anjali Gopalan
Pranaadhika Sinha at Elaan
Mirna Guha at OBO
Dr Anjali Chhabria
Urvashi Butalia
Anita Roy
Pramada Menon
The Margaret Sanger Center International at Planned Parenthood of New York City
Raju and Lata Bharti

Invaluable, informative guides:

The Hite Report by Shere Hite

Ready or Not? by Tina Radziszewicz

www.scarleteen.com – owned and operated by Heather Corinna

Intimate Relations by Sudhir Kakar

Indebted to:

Neelini Sarkar

V.K Karthika

Amy Levine

Much love and appreciation to:

Gulumasi and Prikshat Uncle

Nora Alogna and Ed Chowdhury

Kavita Bhanot

The Sawhneys – Shiv, Rama, Aarti, Susan, Vik and Margarita, for their generosity, love and kindness.

The Wasons – my mother Jyoti, for raising me with freedom and friendship; my father Harish, for believing in me before I did; my brother Rajeev; my brother Sanjeev; and Jonathan, for endless love and support.

Above all, Hirsh Sawhney for bringing true love and happiness into my life.

Index

READ MORE FROM HARPERCOLLINS INDIA

Choose from a new and exciting range of titles for young adults

HARPER

Extreme American Makeover

Mitali Perkins

She's short, she's spunky, she's just a regular girl

Sameera—Sparrow to her friends—is used to feeling invisible. But all that is about to change. As her father's presidential campaign heats up, Sameera trades in her summer vacation for a crash course in becoming a celebrity. Step 1: Fabulous Makeover, of course!

As it turns out, the makeover *is* amazing. But some of the campaign staff aren't content with a trendy haircut, stilettos and designer outfits. They've decided to package Pakistan-born, plain-speaking Sameera as 'Sammy' Righton—a giggly, carefree, all-American girl. No more wearing comfy jeans and sneakers, dancing the bhangra or blogging from the heart—in other words, Sameera must forget about being herself.

What they don't know is that Sameera has a mind of her own. And plenty to say. Not to mention a gutsy, straight-talking blog that could go live to millions…

Potato Chips

Anshuman Mohan

'We students are like potatoes... Only the finest of us will get made into chips!'

When Aman Malhotra is made to change schools, he knows that his goose is well and truly cooked. From the easygoing, friendly atmosphere of Akshar, he is thrust into the big, bad world of St Xavier's. The reason, according to his parents: a big school prepares you much better for your future, i.e., IIT. Things, Aman realizes, are about to change and not for the better. The progress graph of his life plunges downwards in a sudden freefall—his grades suffer, his classmates snicker at him, his teachers think he is a brat.

Struggling to make sense of his new, high-pressure surroundings, Aman casts his net far and wide for friends and finds Shubho, a boy with a crafty drop-shot and a mean backhand. As Aman gets to know Shubho and tries to help him out, he also begins to get his own life back on track. A hero, he finally understands, comes in the most unlikely of guises and isn't necessarily the most popular kid in school.

An honest, in-your-face story of school life and adolescence—the highs, the lows, the pranks, the exams, the friendships, the fights—Potato Chips is crisp and smart, fresh and funny.

How to Salsa in a Sari

Dona Sarkar

Issa Mazumder, a nerdy half Indian, half African teenage girl who lives in the US with her single mother, has just been utterly destroyed because the gorgeous Cat Morena, Latina princess, Issa's worst enemy and the most popular girl in school, has stolen Issa's equally nerdy boyfriend Adam. And there's worse to come – Issa's mother announces that she and Cat's father are getting married. And they are moving into Cat's huge mansion.

Cat has no respect for Issa's traditions and makes Issa's life hell. But Issa gets some tough advice: if she wants Cat Morena to welcome her traditions, Issa had better learn to salsa in a sari!